THE MOTIVATION MYTH

The
MOTIVATION
Myth

How High Achievers Really
Set Themselves Up to Win

JEFF HADEN

PORTFOLIO / PENGUIN

Portfolio/Penguin
An imprint of Penguin Random House LLC
375 Hudson Street
New York, New York 10014

Most Portfolio books are available at a discount when purchased in quantity for sales promotions or corporate use. Special editions, which include personalized covers, excerpts, and corporate imprints, can be created when purchased in large quantities. For more information, please call (212) 572-2232 or e-mail specialmarkets@penguinrandomhouse.com. Your local bookstore can also assist with discounted bulk purchases using the Penguin Random House corporate Business-to-Business program. For assistance in locating a participating retailer, e-mail B2B@penguinrandomhouse.com.

Library of Congress Cataloging-in-Publication Data

Names: Haden, Jeff (William Jeffrey), 1960- author.
Title: The motivation myth : how high achievers really set
themselves up to win / Jeff Haden.
Description: New York : Portfolio, [2018] | Includes index.
Identifiers: LCCN 2018001906| ISBN 9780399563768 (hardcover) |
ISBN 9780399563782 (epub)
Subjects: LCSH: Motivation (Psychology) |
Personality and motivation. | Success.
Classification: LCC BF503 .H328 2018 | DDC 153.8--dc23
LC record available at https://lccn.loc.gov/2018001906

Printed in the United States of America
5 7 9 10 8 6 4

Book design by Daniel Lagin

Portions of this book were revised from content that was originally published on Inc.com.

To everyone who hasn't achieved their dreams—yet.

CONTENTS

CONTENTS

ACKNOWLEDGMENTS

There's an old saying, "You never want to meet people you admire because in real life they will only disappoint." In the last few years I've met dozens of incredibly successful people and found that nothing could be further from the truth.

A famished Richard Branson apologized for having a sandwich delivered during our interview; then he offered me half, saying he wouldn't be able to eat unless I joined him. Metallica guitarist Kirk Hammett's management rep told me we had twenty minutes max for our interview. Kirk winked at me and did forty great minutes. Then he hung out and met other *Inc.* staffers. Then he invited my wife and me to see the band perform at Webster Hall. (Best show ever.) Seven-time NASCAR champion Jimmie Johnson sat down to talk, even though he was two hours past his scheduled departure time, because he knew

ACKNOWLEDGMENTS

I had waited. (And then he set me up with his triathlon trainer, Jamey Yon.)

Actor Clive Standen fills every moment of his workday so that when he is home, he's *home.* His definition of success is being a good husband and father. Joe Gibbs, Super Bowl–winning coach and NASCAR championship team owner, gave every member of the video crew a signed copy of his book *Game Plan for Life* because he hoped it would make a small difference in people's lives. Dany Garcia, who with Dwayne "The Rock" Johnson cofounded Seven Bucks Productions, spent more time asking me what *I* do to be more focused and productive and how to accomplish multiple goals. She already knows what she knows; she wanted to know what *I* know.

Venus Williams is . . . well, Venus is absolutely delightful.

Mark Cuban stopped to chat with an unpaid intern who had spent six hours stuck in a chair at the far end of a lonely hallway. Eric Ripert hung out in the kitchen of Le Bernardin after a video shoot and talked shop; later, he treated my wife and me to the best meal we've ever had. Lance Armstrong is a guy I'd love to have a few beers with (and I don't like beer). Actor Robert Patrick answered all my questions and then spent half an hour finding out about me. After learning that I live in Virginia, he said, "Hey, Bobby [Robert] Duvall lives there. The next time I'm up that way, let's all get together." (Hey, Robert: Gladly!) NASCAR team owner Rick Hendrick (who also owns more than a hundred automobile dealerships) shook his head when I thanked him for taking the time to speak, and said, "I have nothing more important to do right now than talk to you." And I genuinely believe he meant it.

Dale Earnhardt Jr. reorganized his jam-packed New York City media day schedule so we could shoot a video interview together. Def Leppard guitarist Phil Collen is a great musician and an even nicer guy. If it's possible to be a more humble and self-deprecating multi-platinum artist and Grammy Award winner than Zedd, I would love to meet that person. Roger Penske focuses so hard on the little things that you would think he owned only one rental truck, not multiple businesses that generate $26 billion in annual revenue. If I was playing the "What three people, living or dead, would you most like to have dinner with?" game, actor James Purefoy is in my top three. (Hey, James: I'll buy!)

Thanks to each of you, along with others too numerous to mention, for being so generous with your time and your insights. And most of all, thanks for proving what many people unfortunately choose not to believe: that if you are willing to work hard and stay the course, who you are is more than enough for you to become who you really want to be.

Thanks also to my agent, Katie Kotchman, for believing in me before I did. Thanks to my editor, Leah Trouwborst, for doing exactly what I hoped: She dramatically improved my original idea and, better yet, made me think. The incredible team at Penguin Random House have proven, over and over again, that I chose the best publishing house in the world.

ACKNOWLEDGMENTS

Special thanks to Eric Schurenberg, president and editor in chief of *Inc.,* my online home, who has supported me through thick and thin. You may be the boss, but when I think of you, the first word that comes to mind is "friend." Without Eric and everyone at *Inc.,* this book would not have been possible.

Most of all, thanks to my kids, who are already better people than I could ever hope to be, and especially to my wife, Cynthia. Maybe the old saying "behind every great man is a great woman" is occasionally true, but not in my case. Far ahead of this decidedly average man is a great woman. I'm sorry you have to drag me along . . . but I am eternally thankful that you do.

THE MOTIVATION MYTH

INTRODUCTION

You Can Do—and *Be*—
So Much More Than You Think

When I worked in manufacturing for R.R. Donnelley, the world's largest commercial printer, I desperately—and I do mean desperately—wanted to become a plant manager; the closest I came was running manufacturing operations for a small, privately owned company. I spent years trying to get one—just one—short story published; the closest I came was . . . Well, I never came close. (Looking back, deservedly so.) I have dozens of failures to my name. I've tried and failed, over and over.

Even worse, I've let many goals go without even trying to achieve them. I thought about them, I dreamed about them, I imagined what it would feel like to accomplish them . . . but I never even got started.

In both scenarios, I spent a lot of time trying to motivate myself. I'd been told success was all about mind-set, and I wanted to lock in the optimal psychological state before the rubber met the road. We can all remember those times when we were hit with a lightning bolt of inspiration, whether to work out or to start learning French—and we can also remember how that urge never produced any action.

I was in the grip of an insidious myth. I thought motivation was a prerequisite to starting a tedious learning process—a spark necessary to get me going. But motivation is really a result. Motivation is the fire that starts burning after you manually, painfully, coax it into existence, and it feeds on the satisfaction of seeing yourself make progress. The problem with waiting for motivation to strike is that it almost never comes with enough voltage to actually get you started.

Granted, sometimes motivation strikes like a hammer. Minutes or hours later, though, you've lost your enthusiasm, partly because a lightning-bolt burst of motivation is like a sugar rush: It feels great but is impossible to maintain, and when you come down you actually feel worse. Rah-rah speeches and inspirational quotes and fire-walking challenges (more on those in a minute) may help you picture yourself at the top of the mountain with your arms raised in triumph, but the effect is fleeting. After the glow is gone, you're left standing by yourself at the bottom of that same mountain, hugely intimidated by all the steps you need to climb.

So you sit, and dwell, and sulk, and wish, and hope, and maybe even think about saving up for Tony Robbins's next seminar . . . but even that sounds too hard.

HOW SUCCESSFUL PEOPLE APPROACH MOTIVATION

I've met plenty of successful people. Yes, many of them are smart. Yes, some of them are creative. Yes, they're often talented. But none of those traits is crucial to their success. The gene cards we are dealt are just a starting point; nearly every successful person I know started on the downside of advantage. Humble beginnings can create the perfect foundation for success, because starting at the bottom creates almost endless opportunities to enjoy small successes.

Confused? That's okay. The key is to understand how motivation works.

There is only one recipe for gaining motivation: success.

Specifically, the dopamine hits we get when we observe ourselves making progress.

Not huge, life-changing successes. Those come all too infrequently, if ever. If you want to stay motivated, if you want to stay on track, if you want to keep making progress toward the things you hope to achieve, the key is to enjoy small, seemingly minor successes—but on a regular basis. If you're trying to learn a language, it's fun when you realize you can count to twenty. If you're trying to learn an instrument, it's fun when you realize you can read simple sheet music. If you're trying to learn to code, it's fun to realize that silly little program you wrote actually works. Small successes are fun—and motivating.

3

That's why you already have everything you need.

That's why motivation isn't something you *have*. Motivation is something you get, from yourself, automatically, from feeling good about achieving small successes.

Success is a process. Success is repeatable and predictable. Success has less to do with hoping and praying and strategizing than with diligently doing (after a little strategizing, sure): doing the right things, the right way, over and over and over.

It's easy to look back on a path to greatness and assume that every vision was clear, every plan was perfect, every step was executed flawlessly, and tremendous success was a foregone conclusion.

It wasn't. Every extremely successful person I know never expected to achieve as much as they have. (Many still can't believe it.) Almost to a person, one day they woke up and were stunned to see how far they had come.

Why were they so surprised by their success? They were busy doing. They didn't focus on what they did not have. They focused on doing the work, day after day after day, to get them to where they hoped to go.

When you consistently do the right things, success is predictable. Success is inevitable. You just can't think about it too much. No obsessing allowed.

THE RELATIONSHIP BETWEEN HAPPINESS AND SUCCESS

The motivation myth makes us unhappy for two reasons. First, it leads to a sin of commission. A person who self-identifies as a failure, who regularly quits before reaching the finish line, is a chronically unhappy person. But it also causes a sin of omission. We aren't mindfully enjoying one of the most rewarding experiences on earth: slowly growing stronger, or more skillful, or more wise.

Like when my grandfather bought a racehorse.

I wasn't even a teenager, but even I knew it was a terrible decision. A racehorse was a luxury he and my grandmother surely could not afford. But at least ongoing costs were low because he lived on a farm. That's a justification I'm sure he floated by my grandmother.

Over the next year he would scrape together entry fees and race the horse with little success at small local tracks. One was no better than an open field rutted by the pounding of hooves. Another featured an announcer who placed his PA system on the back of his truck and powered it with a generator that almost drowned out the sound of his voice. (I can still remember him saying, "As you folks know, in Virginia it's illegal to bet at a racetrack . . . but if you folks mosey away from the track and on down to that big old oak tree over yonder, I'm sure someone will be happy to accommodate you." And I can still remember the muscles in my father's face tightening in response.)

Then one day the impossible happened. After somehow talking one of the better jockeys into riding his horse—"somehow" surely including slipping the man an extra forty dollars, a princely sum for the ride—his horse placed second at the now long-defunct Goochland Races, held at the county fairgrounds less than ten miles from where my grandfather lived.

After the race, he stood at the finish line and held up the small silver plate so we could take his picture. Then we led the horse back around the sandy track toward the barn area as some of the people on the outside of the rail congratulated him.

I was only twelve, but even I could see a noticeable difference in the way he walked. For those moments he stood taller, carrying himself with a clear sense of accomplishment, dignity, and pride.

Only years later did I realize why my grandfather had bought the horse. He desperately wanted to be someone. He wanted to matter.

That's a wish we all share. For the most part, that's why we change careers, or start businesses, or play an instrument, or go back to school. That's why we run for local office, volunteer at a charity, or are active in church.

We want to matter . . . but when we focus solely on mattering to other people—when we focus on seeing the reflection of our worth in the eyes of others—the difference that feeling makes in our lives is often fleeting.

By the time we got back to the farm, my grandfather's glow had faded. Sure, he was still happy, but all the external benefits of that small success—the smiles, the words of congratulation, the nods from friends and strangers—had disappeared.

At the end of my grandfather's racing journey, he was left with what we are all left with, no matter what we have accomplished and no matter how much praise or recognition we have received from others. The accomplishment, no matter how amazing, is just the cherry on top of the fulfillment cake.

If your goal has long been to build a business that does $10 million in sales, you feel amazing the second you hit that target—but that moment of achievement is just one moment. If your goal has long been to run a marathon, you feel amazing the second you cross the finish line—but that moment of achievement is just one moment.

The road to a target, to a goal, or to a finish line is filled with countless hours of work and determination and sacrifice . . . and countless opportunities to feel good about what you have accomplished, each and every day along the way.

A slice of satisfaction, fulfillment, and happiness can be found in the achievement . . . but the real source of consistent, lasting happiness lies in the process. My grandfather wasn't involved in the process. Granted, he bought the horse . . . but then

he jumped to the end. He skipped all the steps in between: training the horse, conditioning the horse, developing the horse's speed
slowly but surely, teaching it not just how to run but how to race.

He didn't give himself the chance to enjoy the daily doses of
fulfillment that come from engaging in the process. Accomplishing something, no matter how small the task, makes us feel better about ourselves. That's why to-do lists are so popular. (Many
people write down really easy tasks—or tasks they've already
completed—just so they can scratch them off.)

Incredibly successful people set a goal and then focus all
their attention on the process necessary to achieve that goal.
They set a goal and then, surprisingly, they forget the goal.

Sure, the goal is still out there. But what they care about
most is what they need to do today—and when they accomplish
that, they are happy about today. They feel good about today.

They feel good about themselves because they've accomplished what they set out to do today, and that sense of accomplishment gives them all the motivation they need to do what
they need to do when tomorrow comes—because success, even
tiny, incremental success, is the best motivational tool of all.

When you savor the small victories, you get to feel good
about yourself every day, because you no longer feel compelled
to compare the distance between here and there. You don't have
to wait for "someday" to feel good about yourself; if you do what
you planned to do today, you're a winner.

When I was training for long cycling events, I often rode up mountains. I've always hated the climbs . . . but I loved completing them, and years later I still love knowing I completed them. Think about anything you've done that was extremely hard, and how you felt afterward, and you'll know exactly what I mean.

For years I missed out on the happiness and fulfillment that come from accomplishing all the little steps in my various goal-achievement (actually, goal-failure) journeys.

You don't have to.

But it won't be easy. Success—lasting, fulfilling, meaningful success—never is.

Want to start a business? Don't be fooled by the work-at-home hype. Launching a successful business will make you wonder what the words "free time" could possibly mean.

Want to rise to the top of your organization? Don't be fooled by the work-life-balance fluff. Tremendous effort and dedication are required.

Want to run a marathon? Forget some sixty-day shortcut system that promises maximum results from minimal input. Life doesn't work that way.

To accomplish anything worthwhile, and especially to achieve a goal others say is impossible, you have to work your ass off. There are no shortcuts. The only way is the hard way.

Yet there are plenty of ways to make the process fun. There are plenty of ways to make the process uplifting. There are plenty of ways to enjoy every step of the journey . . . as well as that final step onto your personal podium.

Want to be happier? Want to be more successful at everything you choose to pursue? The paths to both happiness and success are one and the same.

You don't need to wait until you can find more time; you have all the time you need. You don't need to wait until you can find more money; money never drives success. (Though if you so choose, money can be the result of success.) And you absolutely do not need more motivation.

You don't need to wait to find your passion; if you follow this book's program, your passions—plural intended, as you'll soon see—will find you.

You will stand strong. You won't back off. You won't back down. You'll make smart decisions. You won't focus on what you don't have, because what you *do* have—however little it may seem—is more than enough.

And you will find that the process, not just the result but the *process* involved in becoming something that you once dreamed of, will also make you feel awesome about yourself—each and every day.

Some people are successful. Some people are happy.

You can be both.

Here's how.

CHAPTER 1

Motivation Is Not the Spark

A key moment in Tony Robbins's "Unleash the Power Within" seminar occurs when participants take part in the fire walk.

(Okay, it's more like a "kinda-hot coals" walk, but "fire" sounds more dangerous and macho and Katy Perry "Roar"-y. After all, Tony does know a little something about branding.)

(Actually, Tony knows a *lot* about branding.)

(And actually, this is the last time I'll take a shot at Tony. I think.)

Robbins describes the fire walk as "a symbolic experience that proves if you can make it through the fire, you can make it through anything."* The premise sounds great: Walking across

---

*Falyn Page, "Tony Robbins Hot Coal Walk Injures Dozens, Authorities Say," CNN, June 27, 2016, www.cnn.com/2016/06/24/us/tony-robbins-hot-coal-walkers-burned/index.html.

kinda-hot coals gives you lasting confidence and motivation by tapping into the amazing power lying dormant within you.

In fact, it doesn't.

Fire-walking is a one-off event. Fire-walking is like listening to a motivational speech: You go home inspired and excited and all jazzed up . . . but you wake up the next day the same person you were the day before, *because you haven't truly accomplished anything.*

(Except listen. And pay for the seminar.)

Most people are confused about the source of motivation. They think motivation is the spark that automatically produces lasting eagerness to do hard work; the greater the motivation, the more effort you're willing to put in.

Actually, motivation is a *result*. Motivation is the pride you take in work you have already done—which fuels your willingness to do even more.

That's why tips for how to feel more motivated often fall short. Most of that advice can be boiled down to "You *can* be more motivated. All you have to do is dig deep into your mind and find that motivation within."

(And burn your feet a little.)

The same is true for confidence, confidence being closely linked to motivation. The thinking goes, "You can be more confident. All you have to do is *decide* to be more confident." It's easy: Suppress negative thoughts, suppress negative perspectives, repeat some really cool self-affirmational statements, and . . . presto! I'm like Tony Robbins.

Or not.

The main problem in both cases is the way we've come to think about motivation.

Most definitions of "motivation" involve some phrase like "the force or influence that causes someone to do something." Motivation is viewed as a spark, a precondition, a prerequisite, a pre*something* that is required before we can start. If we aren't motivated, we can't start. If we aren't motivated, we can't *do*.

Bullshit.

Real motivation comes *after* you start. Motivation isn't the result of hearing a speech or watching a movie or crisping your soles. Motivation isn't passive; motivation is active.

HOW TO START WHEN YOU'RE 0 PERCENT MOTIVATED

The best way to get motivated is to break a sweat, literally or symbolically.

Getting started is often the hardest part. Financial planners frequently recommend paying off a small debt first, even though the balance on that bill may carry the lowest interest rate of all your debts. Rationally, that approach makes no sense: If you carry a balance on three credit cards, the card you pay off first should be the one with the highest interest rate. But the thought of paying off, say, a $7,000 balance when you can spare only an extra $200 a month . . . ugh. The time horizon is too long for the payoff—literally—to seem worth it. The "irrational" approach often works better: Working to pay off the card with the smallest balance seems a lot more attainable. Once you start, you can see the difference. Knocking $200 off an $800 debt feels like you've accomplished something. After next month, you're halfway done! And once you pay off that card, you'll be motivated to keep going to pay off the next card.

Think about why you sometimes procrastinate. (Don't say you never put things off. Show me someone who doesn't procrastinate and I'll show you a robot. *Everyone* procrastinates.)

I definitely procrastinate.

One example: I've written more than seven million published words. (Please keep the jokes about long-windedness to yourself.) You might then assume it's easy for me to sit down and write, but at times it's anything but: I'll make calls, take care of administrative tasks, do a little "research" (in my line of work, any reading is research, right?), play with the cats . . . I love to write, but sometimes the thought of writing seems daunting, especially at the beginning of a project, when I need to find the right voice and the best way into the material.

Except for the cats, I can rationalize that I'm being productive, but usually I'm just procrastinating.

Another example: I like to ride bicycles. Over the last five or six years I've ridden about 35,000 miles. I love riding, but sometimes I'll do *anything* not to ride.

Neither makes sense, right? Writing and riding are both things I love to do, yet at times I find ways to actively avoid doing them. Putting off tasks I *don't* enjoy would make a lot more sense.

I love to ride my bike, but sometimes the thought of riding seems daunting, especially those first few miles, when it's cold outside and my legs are stiff and my heart has just started to pound. I pant and gasp and wonder why I'm on the stupid bike . . . but then something magical happens. Somehow my aversion to "hard" goes away once I break a sweat.

The endorphins kick in. My legs warm up. I feel proud that I can do something hard, and do it reasonably well. That rush of satisfaction I always feel? (That rush of satisfaction you always feel when you start doing something you've put off . . . and suddenly realize it wasn't as daunting as you anticipated?) I know that feeling will come. I've trained myself to anticipate that natural "high." Instead of thinking, "Ugh. This is going to be hard," I've taught myself to think, "I can't wait for that little high I'll feel when I move from inactivity to activity. I can't wait to feel that rush I know I'll feel when I'm actually doing what I planned to do."

The key is to enjoy the feeling of success that comes from

improving in some small way . . . and then rinse and repeat, over and over again.

Why? Improving feels good. Improving breeds confidence. Improving creates a feeling of competence, and competence breeds self-confidence. Success—in your field or sometimes in any field—breeds motivation. It feels good to improve . . . so you naturally want to keep improving.

You've probably put off a task, finally gotten started . . . and then, once you got started, thought, "I don't know why I kept putting this off. It's going really well. And it didn't turn out to be nearly as hard as I imagined."

And here's the thing: *It never is.*

Why? Because once you get started, once you get active and start doing something—doing not just anything but something you know will get you one step closer to your goal—the process gets easier. Motivation kicks in because you've gotten started. A really cool virtuous cycle—one we'll look at in detail a little later—kicks in. You feel good because you're engaged and in- volved.

You feel motivated because you took action. Motivation is a result, not a precondition. You don't need motivation to break a sweat. Break a sweat and you'll feel motivated.

Once you start, it's easy to keep going. The act of getting out of the house to go for a jog is often harder than actually running the five miles you planned. The act of sitting down at your desk to start writing a proposal is often harder than putting together twenty pages of material. The act of picking up your phone is often harder than cold-calling twenty prospects.

Starting is hard because "motivation" doesn't make it easy to start. Starting provides the motivation to finish.

Fire walks don't provide lasting motivation. *Breaking a sweat* provides lasting motivation.

Speeches don't provide lasting motivation. *Progress* provides lasting motivation.

Posters don't provide lasting motivation. *Success* provides lasting motivation.

If you aren't achieving your goals, a lack of motivation or confidence isn't the problem. A lack of motivation or confidence is actually the means to a solution. When you accept your weak points, when you accept your flaws, when you accept your imperfections . . . *that's* when you can motivate yourself to make changes and improve.

Hide from your weaknesses, and you'll always be weak. Accept your weaknesses and work to improve them, and you'll eventually be stronger—and more motivated to keep improving.

But you have to do the right things in order to make real improvements. In upcoming chapters I'll show you how.

Before we do that, though, let's debunk some other myths that have held you back.

Shortcuts Never Get You Where You Really Want to Go

You know this now, but it bears repeating: Lightning bolts of inspiration strike only in the movies—or in the minds of people who want to believe they're capable of inspiring you (if you pay for the privilege, of course).

Wait for a sudden burst of inspiration and you'll never get started . . . and if you do manage to ride that initial sugar-rush wave, you'll never stick with it, because sugar rushes never last.

The same is true for seeking shortcuts. You can't "hack" your way to success.

I love Tim Ferriss, but don't fool yourself: He works *incredibly* hard. The real premise of *The 4-Hour Workweek* is to increase your output by ten times per hour. Tim is the first to admit he has no problem with hard work—the key is to apply your hard work to the right things. But somehow that premise has been twisted to become "I just need to find the secret (something) that results in instant success."

Of course there are no hacks. Sure, you can learn to peel a banana a lot more effectively (thanks, Tim!), but real success, *meaningful* success, is never instant. You absolutely should look for better, more effective ways to accomplish your goal—and I'll show you several—but there are no shortcuts.

There definitely aren't for me.

I'm as insecure as anyone I know. Where feeling confident

and self-assured is concerned, on a scale of one to one hundred, one hundred being Oprah, I'm a one.

So some years ago when I was invited to speak to an audience of around 1,000 people, my first thought was "Yes!" My second thought was "Oh no!" I had never spoken to an audience larger than about 150 people. Plus, I had been asked to speak on an unfamiliar topic.

Even so, the opportunity was too good to pass up. So I looked around and found a few articles with tips on how to captivate a large audience; it seemed all I needed to do was employ some big nonverbal gestures and speak more loudly at some points and softly at others, and boom: I'd kill.

Nope. I bombed.

Granted, everyone told me I did fine. (To a speaker, being told you were "fine" is like being a teenager who is told he has a good personality.) Sure, I wanted to believe them. I wanted desperately to ignore my feelings of incompetence, disappointment, and failure.

And then I realized I would never get better if I didn't (1) accept the fact that I had failed and (2) work really hard to improve. So I went back to the drawing board. I wrangled invitations to local civic groups. I spoke to students at local colleges. I forced myself to speak on topics outside my wheelhouse so I could learn the mechanics of crafting a great hook and a great story.

Sometimes I did well, sometimes I did poorly, but over time I gained competence and skill.

Am I still nervous before I step out in front of a large crowd? Oh, hell yeah. I'm a hot mess of insecurity. But I can work through those feelings, not because I engage in a lot of happy horseshit self-talk and fire-walking bravado but because I know I've been there, done that, and can do it again. I'm confident because I have success in my pocket. I'm confident because I've done the work.

Confidence comes from preparation. Hesitation, anxiety, fear . . . Those feelings don't come from some deep, dark, irrational place inside you. The anxiety you feel—the lack of confidence you feel—comes from feeling unprepared. Once you realize that you can prepare yourself, that you can develop techniques to do whatever you seek to do well, that whatever you hope to achieve is ultimately a craft that you can learn to do better and better and better, and that any skills you currently lack you can learn, you naturally become more confident as you become more prepared.

Take Jamie Little, a pit reporter for Fox Sports and the first woman to accomplish several motor sports broadcasting milestones.

"When my mom and I moved to Las Vegas," she says, "I met Carey Hart [motocross racer, freestyle motocross competitor, married to Pink]. He had a big influence on me. I thought he was the coolest thing ever. I already had a thing for motorcycles, and

I learned about Supercross through him. I would take dirt-bike magazines to class with me. . . . I loved it. It was my happy world.

"I went up to a guy working for ESPN at a race and said, 'How do I get started?' He let me hang out for two years with no pay so I could get my work known. I learned to write; I learned to interview athletes. . . . It was a great training ground. I wasn't getting paid, but that was okay."

But that doesn't mean her path was easy. When Jamie started working for ESPN covering NASCAR races, the challenges only increased.

"I don't think there was anything harder I could have taken on than covering NASCAR at that level," she says. "I look back and wonder where I got the courage. I was coming into this garage; there weren't a whole lot of people before me that had done it, especially not women. . . . I had to figure things out on my own, which was the best way but also the most challenging way.

"My confidence came from overpreparing. I still overprepare. I put together a page of notes for every driver, talk to the drivers and crew chiefs at the track . . . and then I use all that to help me trim the fat down to the most pertinent facts and the best angles to share with viewers during the broadcast. I use that same approach with other forms of racing. Feeling overprepared lets me feel confident and natural."

And where does the drive required to help you prepare come from? Success—small, frequent, repeat successes.

It truly is a virtuous cycle.

Confidence is a feeling, but ultimately confidence is the result of knowing that you're not only willing to do the work, but that you actually will *do* the work. You won't try to hack your way to success.

Hacking is great when you need to perform a simple task. Hacking is worthless when you need to acquire a complex skill or accomplish a huge goal. Plus, hacking doesn't provide a jolt of motivation like gaining skill and expertise does. And hacking doesn't help you gain confidence in your ability to accomplish other big goals—whereas real success in one pursuit can yield greater confidence and motivation in other areas of life.

Take me again: The first major Gran Fondo I rode (a Gran Fondo is a mass-participation cycling event) was one hundred miles long and featured more than eleven thousand feet of climbing over four mountains. Two of those climbs were on dirt and gravel roads. It was long. It was endless. It was physically and emotionally harder than just about anything I had ever done. But I finished it.

And for weeks afterward I felt more confident. I worried less about what people thought of me. I had done something huge, at least for me, and the memory of that accomplishment carried me for a long time.

Of course, riding the Gran Fondo was the opposite of a fire walk. While it was seemingly a one-off event, that one day was also the culmination of months of hard work. I didn't close my eyes and sprint across semihot coals. My eyes were wide open, every day, to the effort and sacrifice and determination it took to follow the right routine that would allow me to accomplish my goal.

That's why motivation and confidence gained in one aspect of your life can spill over into other aspects of your life. When you feel good about yourself in one way—when you achieve some degree of success in one aspect of your life—you tend to feel better about other parts of your life as well. After all, if you can do one thing well, you can do *lots* of things well. You realize that all you have to do is find the right process, work the process, and enjoy the feeling of success and resulting motivation you get from constant improvement (because if you follow the right process, you will constantly improve).

Plus, many shortcuts shackle you with extra risk in exchange for productivity.

In the music industry, for instance, it's almost a given that artists eventually regret the terms of their first contract; artists are so happy to get signed—and get an advance—that they will sign almost anything. (Tom Petty was so unhappy with his first contract, he sued his label and risked losing his career rather than continue under its terms.)

Joe Satriani took a different course. Joe has sold millions of critically acclaimed solo albums, toured with Mick Jagger, Deep Purple, and Chickenfoot, created signature guitar and equipment lines, founded his own long-running concert series, G3 . . . and, oh yeah, he's been nominated for fourteen Grammys.

Joe told me why he decided to take personal ownership over each part of the publishing process. He was in a band called the Squares in the early 1980s.

"Our rehearsal space was in the same building as Nolo Press, a company that made how-to books with tear-out pages for all sorts of legal situations. Their Dumpster was right outside the door where we would hang out and have a smoke and a drink in between practicing, and it was always overflowing with damaged books. So we're out there wondering how we're ever going to make it in the music business and start absentmindedly flipping through books. One of them showed how to start all kinds of businesses.

"I took it home and was fascinated. I thought the upcoming vacation the band was taking was an opportunity for me to just 'do the book.' I got a real copy of the book and decided I needed to start my own publishing company and my own record company and then make a record. I just followed the advice in the book, filled out the forms, went to the Oakland courthouse and paid my twelve dollars, and suddenly I was a record company owner."

Joe ended up recording an unusual, avant-garde record with no bass, drums, or keyboards. He realized that he "didn't have to go out and chase the brick-and-mortar powers that be." This was during an era when the music business did not have the equal access to opportunity that it has now. "That challenge was what gave me the energy to pursue the future I glimpsed in that little misprint of a book, *How to Start Your Own Business,*" Joe says.

"Then I was in a band rehearsal one day and our bass player said, 'Hey, I think they reviewed your record in *Guitar Player* magazine.'"

Armed with a newfound confidence, Joe slowly made a name for himself. Better yet, he says, "I was a musician who could not be taken advantage of. That's why I wound up owning all my own publishing and making a deal that was quite advantageous for a new solo artist."

Had Joe found a way to get signed by a record label, he might have eased some short-term financial pressure, but he almost surely would have signed away his publishing rights, his control over his art, and his chances for long-term financial success.

Even though taking a shortcut may lead to a short-term success, you will often regret ever having taken it.

Routine Is Not the Last Resort of the Less Talented (or the Boring)

Process gets a bad rap. Hard work, consistent effort, long hours . . . That's what stupid people with no talent do, right?

Um, nope.

Take Michael Ovitz, the guy who built Creative Artists Agency (CAA) into the largest and one of the most powerful organizations in Hollywood. He started in the mail room at William Morris, then the biggest agency in town. Here's what he told James Andrew Miller in the excellent book *Powerhouse: The Untold Story of Hollywood's Creative Artists Agency.*

When I went to William Morris, I decided that I had to do something that was disruptive. I was in the mailroom with about twenty guys. They'd come in at nine, so I came in at seven. They'd leave at six, I'd leave at ten o'clock at night. Some days I left earlier because at that time I was also going to school at night to get my master's in business. I worked my butt off—reading everything there was to read. I was a scavenger. Those guys were waiting to be fed things; I went looking for things. I viewed the mailroom as an education course, period, and was going to move over everyone very quickly. I volunteered for every job and was very aggressive.

Three months into the training program, I had begun to notice that the president of the company would often come back to the office after dinner when everyone else had left, so I made sure to be there and became the only guy sitting at a desk on the first floor. As I figured he would, he asked if I could do a favor for him. I did the favor so well that he asked me to work for him some more. I kept doing it each night until he finally made me his assistant.

Ovitz is incredibly smart. Ovitz went on to almost completely transform the way the talent agency business operates—and in many ways how Hollywood operates.

Yet Ovitz decided that the best way to succeed was to develop a routine and then stick to that routine. He did things no one else would. He didn't just rely on his intelligence and talent to succeed. He didn't wait for his boss to "discover" his talents. He didn't wait to get a promotion—and the raise that comes with it—to work harder and sacrifice more. Ovitz relied on his process.

You Don't Need Other People to Support You

Say you have a huge goal you want to accomplish: a massive, audacious, incredibly challenging, and ultimately worthwhile goal. You think about that goal, dream about that goal, obsess about that goal . . . and talk about it with your friends and family.

That last part can sometimes be a big mistake.

Granted, seeking support makes sense at a surface level. Most people assume they should talk about their dreams and goals in order to receive encouragement. And even if positive reinforcement doesn't work, what about negative reinforcement and that extra jolt of motivation you'll undoubtedly receive from wanting to follow through on a public statement of intent? Surely that will keep you going when times get tough, as times inevitably do?

Nope.

Science agrees with me. Research (see? I sometimes am actually performing research and not just procrastinating) shows that people who talk about their intentions are much less likely to follow through on those intentions. Or if you prefer researcher-speak, "Identity-related behavioral intentions that had been noticed by other people were translated into action less intensively than those that had been ignored."* (I know: You don't prefer researcher-speak.)

Here's an example. Say you want to through-hike the Appalachian Trail, a grueling five- to seven-month trek from Georgia to Maine. You're having dinner with friends and tell them you've decided to walk the entire 2,200 miles.

"Oh, wow!" one exclaims. "That sounds amazing. But won't it be super hard?"

"Indeed, it will," you say with some added bass in your voice. You share what you know about tent sites, shelters, infrequent showers, and the cool trail name you're bound to get. (Trail names are nicknames through-hikers are given—or that the pretentious try to give themselves—partly out of tradition and partly because "Slumber Cat" is a lot easier for near strangers to remember than "Martha.")

---

*Peter M. Gollwitzer et al., "When Intentions Go Public: Does Social Reality Widen the Intention-Behavior Gap?" *Psychological Science* 20, no. 5 (May 1, 2009): 612, http://journals.sagepub.com/doi/abs/10.1111/j.1467-9280.2009.02336.x.

You love talking about the trail. It feels awesome to bask in the glow of people who admire you for wanting to take on such a huge challenge. Even though you're sitting in a restaurant, it feels like you're already on the trail.

It also means you're less likely to someday actually *be* on the trail, because "when other people take notice of an individual's identity-related behavioral intention, this gives the individual a premature sense of possessing the aspired-to identity."*

Or in non-researcher-speak: You already got a huge kick out of people *thinking* of you as a trail hiker . . . so now you're less motivated to actually *be* a trail hiker.

Sounds counterintuitive, right? Aren't we supposed to share our intentions so other people can help support and motivate us?

According to NYU psychologist Peter Gollwitzer, one of the authors of the study, that is not the case.

Gollwitzer thinks the issue lies in our sense of identity. Each of us wants to be certain things, and we naturally declare those intentions, even if we have not yet become those things. Check out Twitter bios if you don't believe me. Thousands of people are motivated, innovative, creative, passionate, and unique—not to mention gurus, ninjas, curators, and connoisseurs.

Describing how I plan to run a marathon and how I bought running shoes and a treadmill (because it's really hot outside and that whole sweating thing is icky) and joined a gym and

---

* Gollwitzer et al., "When Intentions Go Public," 612.

found this cool training plan online certainly makes me feel good . . . but it also makes me feel like I'm already halfway to the finish line even though I haven't jogged a single step.

Declaring what we want to be and how we will get there causes us to feel we are further along the path of becoming who we want to be—even though we have in reality done nothing but talk.*

Have you done that before? I have.

Other people can't motivate us, not really, and definitely not for long. And that's because we can't motivate ourselves, not really, and clearly not for long—otherwise we would achieve every goal we set.

The problem also isn't a lack of willpower, even though conventional wisdom would have us think that greater willpower is what separates the achievers from the dreamers.

Other People Were Not Born with Greater Willpower

You sigh when you hear about a friend who just lost twenty pounds. "That's amazing," you think. "I wish I had that kind of willpower. But I don't."

Or you shake your head when you hear your sister-in-law just got an MBA while working full time and raising two kids.

---

* The way to avoid this phenomenon and harness the support or peer pressure of friends is to talk about the *routine* you plan to follow, not your goal. Say, "I plan to run three miles on Monday, Wednesday, and Friday." *That* works.

"That's amazing," you think. "I wish I had that kind of drive and determination. But I don't."

Or you hear about my wife, who earned an MBA and a master's in nurse anesthesia and became a doctor of nurse anesthesia practice while raising a family. (My wife kicks ass.) "That's amazing," you think. "I wish I had that kind of drive and determination. But I don't."

You're right.

And you're wrong.

Exceptional willpower isn't a quality you are born with, like double-jointed thumbs.

Sure, some people may be more self-disciplined than you. But it's unlikely they were born with some certain special something inside them—instead, they've found ways to make decisions that don't require willpower and determination.

They *seem* to have exceptional willpower, but not because they actually have more. Instead, they've learned how to best use what they have. And as a result, they have what Angela Duckworth calls grit. (Her book *Grit: The Power of Passion and Perseverance* is outstanding.) Duckworth says that what really drives success is not "genius" but a combination of passion and long-term perseverance.

My definition of "grit" is: the ability to work hard and respond resiliently to failure and adversity; the inner quality that enables individuals to work hard and stick to their long-term passions and goals.

That definition almost perfectly describes qualities every successful person possesses, because mental toughness builds the foundations for long-term success. Successful people are great at delaying gratification. Successful people are great at withstanding temptation. Successful people are great at overcoming fear in order to do what they need to do. (Of course, that doesn't mean they aren't scared; that means they're brave. There's a huge difference.) Successful people don't just prioritize; they consistently keep doing what they have decided is most important.

All those qualities require what appears to be incredible willpower—but then again, they don't.

Sound impossible? It's not. Later I'll show you how to avoid exercising almost any willpower at all.

You Absolutely Don't Need to Find Your Passion First

I know what you're thinking.

"Wonderful. You've spoken to large groups. And you've ridden a Gran Fondo. That's fine . . . but what if my goal is a *huge* goal? What then, big boy?"

Good question.

Pretend you're Kirk Hammett. (Yes, I'm fascinated by guitarists. Sue me.) You play lead guitar for Metallica, a band that has sold more than 110 million albums. And has won eight

Grammys. And even though the band has been around for thirty years, it's still incredibly popular: In 2016 Metallica performed the first rock concert held at U.S. Bank Stadium in Minneapolis, selling out all 66,000-plus seats in ten minutes. Metallica is arguably the most successful hard rock band in, well, ever.

So if you're Kirk, what do you tell me when I ask about how you got started?

"I wasn't motivated by a lot of the things that might motivate people, like fame or fortune or whatever," he says. "I was motivated by wanting to play the guitar well."

Kirk didn't want to be a rock star. He wanted to play guitar. The goal was, in an odd way, actually the process.

"So one day," he says, "I pulled my guitar out of the closet where it had been sitting for a while and said, 'I'm going to learn how to play you.' I struggled like everyone does, but then I learned to play a few things and I got such a big kick out of that.

"That made me want to keep learning. Over time all those little successes built and built and before long all I wanted to do was play guitar and learn how to play it as well as I possibly could, and I knew that if I just kept working I would keep getting better."

Oh yeah: Kirk is ranked eleventh on *Rolling Stone* magazine's "100 Greatest Guitarists" list.

Kirk sums it up this way: "All it really takes is a desire to keep on doing it. Finding a passion comes from sticking with it, and that is easy when you work hard to keep getting better. And before long, you realize you've gotten passionate about the passion."

Kirk's point about passion is important. It's easy, and extremely tempting when you're rationalizing your own lack of success, to assume successful people have some intangible quality—ideas, talent, drive, skills, creativity, etc.—that you don't have.

In fact that's rarely true. Talent typically reveals itself only in hindsight.

Success is never assured. It looks inevitable only after it is achieved.

Sure, other people may have skills you don't have—at least not yet—but you have skills other people don't have. You don't need a gift. You just need yourself and a willingness to put in a tremendous amount of hard work, effort, and perseverance, because that is where talent comes from.

Winning Medals Doesn't Feel That Good

I once asked Lance Armstrong what he missed about being a professional cyclist.

"The one thing I truly loved about being a pro cyclist was the process," he said. "Not the accolades, not the money, not the podium . . . I miss the process of getting to the point where you can stand on that top step.

"I miss the hours spent alone and suffering and working to get to the point where I could win. I *loved* the process. I loved all the thinking, all the collaborating, all the planning and effort and working with great people. I feel like I got paid to do the races, meet sponsor obligations.... That's what they paid me for. I would have trained for free.

"I don't really miss the result. I miss the work."

When you put in the time and effort, when you make improvements, when you gain a certain level of skill, you become the thing that you're trying to achieve.

"Becoming" feels wonderful because you've earned it.

Say you're a manager of a department; at first you think about managing, but over time you think of yourself as a manager. Leading is no longer only something you do; leading is who you are. Or say you're Kirk Hammett. At first you play a guitar, but in time you think of yourself as a musician.

The same is true in any pursuit; in time you "become" the thing you do. If you've just started jogging, you would never call yourself a runner, but over time—and with improvement—you begin to feel as if you belong to the running community . . . and it's like you give yourself permission to think of yourself not as someone who runs but as a *runner*.

You don't just start a business; you're an *entrepreneur*. You don't just write; you're an *author*.

You don't just strive for success; you're *successful*.

And oddly enough, even though "becoming" is incredibly

motivating, when you transform yourself into a leader or an entrepreneur or a runner or a musician or whatever you hope to be, you no longer need motivation.

You don't have to find the motivation or willpower; you do what you need to do *because that's who you are.*

Hopefully you see where this is going. Each little success is motivating. Each little success gives you confidence. The accumulation of small successes makes the process, um, maybe not fun, but definitely rewarding—and that's all you need to keep going.

And somehow, without noticing when it happens, you stop thinking about following your routine for three months or six months or a year. You just think about that day and what you will do that day. Somehow, without noticing when it happens, you embrace the routine and not the goal. Every day you get to feel good about yourself, and that sense and feeling of accomplishment motivates you to do it all over again the next day.

In short, the process looks like this:

Success ➔ Motivation ➔ More Success ➔ More Motivation ➔ More Success = *Becoming*

Knowing you've done what you set out to do, no matter how small—or silly—it may be, taps into the storehouse of motivation you already have inside you.

Earned success is the best motivational tool of all. That feeling, that knowledge, is hugely energizing because it's based not on wishing and hoping and dreaming but on a reality—a reality you created.

So forget the fire-walking. Forget the self-talk. Forget searching for, or paying for, the right kind of motivation. Tony is right in one way: All the motivation you need is already inside you. But you won't tap into it by seizing a single moment of inspiration. You won't stay motivated because you experienced one "aha!" moment.

You'll stay motivated when you find a process you trust and commit to working that process for as little as a week. Forget how far you need to go to reach your goal; just commit to following the process for a week.

By the end of that week you'll have made a small improvement: You'll be able to run a little farther, or lift a little more weight, or speak with greater confidence, or perform a task more effectively. Whatever goal you set, you will have moved a few steps closer to achieving that goal.

Never forget that we all lack confidence. We all lack motivation. We all have insecurities, doubts, fears. All of us. We all *say* we want to achieve things, but we don't really want to achieve them unless we are willing to take the necessary steps to achieve what we say we want.

Wanting something badly isn't enough. No matter how badly you may want to achieve something, what matters more—a lot more—than the power of "why" is the power of "how."

We'll talk a lot about "how." For now, just know that as you follow the right routine and gain a small—even very small— measure of skill, your motivation grows, your confidence grows, and your happiness grows, and those qualities make it easy to keep following the right routine, to keep improving, to keep gaining skill and confidence and motivation . . . because you will have earned those feelings.

And in time you will become whatever it is you set out to be.

So yeah, while I love Tony . . . fuck fire walks.

CHAPTER 2

The Greater Your Focus, the Lower Your Chances of Success

Let's say an initial spark—or kinda-hot coal—did manage to get you started. Why didn't you keep going? Why didn't the power of activity, of getting started, of breaking a sweat, fuel the motivation you needed to keep going?

Your process may have been at fault; following a process that doesn't yield short-term results, much less long-term results, is incredibly demotivating. We'll talk about that in upcoming chapters.

But you also may have fallen prey to the myth of focus, which says that the only way to be a high achiever is to regularly remind, coerce, and torture yourself into putting forth effort.

Let's take a step back. Did you get to work on time today? Did you get the kids to their activities on time? Did you get dinner on the table and cut the grass and do the laundry and all the other stuff you needed to do?

Of course you did.

Why? You didn't really have a choice.

Choices present a huge obstacle to meeting our objectives. They deplete our willpower to pick long-term gratification over short-term gratification. As Dr. Travis Bradberry, author of *Emotional Intelligence 2.0*, writes, "Even though we don't always realize it, as the day goes on, we have increased difficulty exerting self-control and focusing on our work. As self-control wears out, we feel tired and find tasks to be more difficult, and our mood sours."[*]

Having too many choices is also a problem. In a classic study, psychologists Sheena Iyengar and Mark Lepper set up a display table with twenty-four varieties of gourmet jam at an upscale food market. Those who sampled the spreads received a coupon for one dollar off any jam. On another day, shoppers saw a similar table, except that only six varieties of jam were on display. The large display attracted more interest than the small one . . . but when the time came to purchase, people who had seen the large display were one-tenth as likely to buy as people who had seen the small display.[†]

Choices are a problem, because choices force you to decide what you *want* to do.

---

[*] Dr. Travis Bradberry, "11 Tweaks to Your Morning Routine Will Make Your Entire Day More Productive," TalentSmart, www.talentsmart.com/articles /11-Tweaks-to-Your-Morning-Routine-Will-Make-Your-Entire-Day-More -Productive-527453707-p-1.html.

[†] Barry Schwartz, "More Isn't Always Better," *Harvard Business Review*, June 2006, https://hbr.org/2006/06/more-isnt-always-better.

What happens when you turn "I want to" into "I have to"? You make it to work on time. Punctuality is nonnegotiable. Getting to work on time is not a goal; it's a task. So is making dinner; you have no choice. So is taking care of your kids; it's nonnegotiable.

Going to the gym, on the other hand, is a goal. We may *want* to work out . . . but we don't *have* to work out. You don't make it to the gym because you can negotiate, if only with yourself, and make other choices.

That's why the power of routine, something we'll look at in detail later, is so important. When you create a routine, embrace that routine, and see the results of that routine, you stop negotiating with yourself. You see your routine as a task, in the best possible way: Your routine isn't something you choose to do; it's just what you do. And you stop making choices that don't support your goals.

Best of all, you stop having to look back and wonder why you didn't follow through on your plans—and why you're still stuck in the same place you've always been.

TO REACH A GOAL, DON'T FOCUS ON THE GOAL

Let's use me as an example again. (I'm the poster child for lessons learned and cautionary tales.)

I love setting huge goals. Unfortunately, my huge goals don't always love me back.

In my twenties I thought it would be cool to run a marathon. I didn't have a burning desire to be a runner; I just imagined all the admiring glances I'd receive when I regaled people with my New York City Marathon stories.

The first day of "training" I jogged about two miles. The next day I jogged two miles. The third day it was really hot, I tweaked my ankle when I sidestepped a Chihuahua with an attitude, and after I finally limped home, I plopped down on the front steps of my house and thought, "Crap. I can barely run two miles. How will I ever run twenty-six miles? That's impossible."

And I gave up.

Of course, you could say I quit because my goal didn't have sufficient personal meaning, and in some ways you would be right. It's really hard to overcome challenges and setbacks when you don't care enough (or, worse, when what you care most about is what other people will think).

But caring, though important, is rarely sufficient. Millions of people sincerely care—about their careers or their health or their families or the environment or politics or a social cause—and yet they still give up long before they manage to achieve a meaningful goal.

Instead, the main problem with setting a huge goal lies much less with caring and much more in two simple words: "here" and "there."

The distance from *here*, where you start, to *there*, where you someday want to be, is too great, especially at the beginning.

For example:

- If your goal is to lose forty pounds, and this week you managed to lose only one pound, how defeating is that? The distance from here to there is too great.
- If your goal is to save a million dollars for retirement, and this month you managed to save only a hundred dollars, how defeating is that? The distance from here to there is too great.
- If your goal is to go back to school and change careers, and you've managed to complete only one class toward a degree, how defeating is that? The distance from here to there is too great.

The distance between your dream and the stark reality of your present is incredibly demoralizing—no wonder you give up on that goal.

Unfortunately, it's a cycle I've repeated more than a few times.

So for Gosh Sakes, Don't Always Keep Your Goal in Mind

Thinking about goals is like thinking about winning the lottery: You get to dream big and imagine yourself living a totally different life.

Dreams are really important. They make us human. We dare to set nearly impossible goals.

Yet all those imaginings are worthless without a process to help us achieve them. A dream, once born, quickly dies without a process to support it.

Then a dream turns into a regret—and all of us already have too many of those.

The key is to set a goal, use it as a target that helps you create a plan for achieving it . . . and then do your best to forget all about that goal. As I learned from James Clear, a leading thinker on the subject, the best use of a goal is to inform the process you will follow to achieve it.

What's the difference between a goal and a process?

- If you're a manager, your *goal* is to develop your employees. Your *process* is how you identify areas for improvement, create implementation plans, follow through on training and coaching and feedback. Your process is what you do to make your goal happen.
- If you're a teacher, your *goal* is to help your students reach their potential. Your *process* is how you craft your lectures, create slides and ancillary materials, find ways to motivate individual students. Your process is what you do to make your goal happen.
- If you're a parent, your *goal* is to raise healthy, happy kids. Your *process* is how you build your children's self-confidence

and self-esteem, nurture their dreams, instill important values. Your process is what you do to make your goal happen.

Take Arnold Schwarzenegger. Before he became a movie star and later the governor of California, Arnold was a six-time Mr. Olympia (the highest achievement in bodybuilding).

As a teenager, he decided he wanted to win the Mr. Olympia contest, but on a daily basis he cared only about reps. In his mind, each repetition of an exercise took him one step closer to becoming Mr. Olympia. At the gym, he wasn't focused on winning the contest; he cared only about doing the reps, about doing the work, about doing what was necessary to get him to his goal.

Sure, he wanted to become Mr. Olympia. He set that goal . . . and then he forgot that goal and focused on reps, and reps, and more reps.*

Everyone has goals. The people who actually achieve their goals create routines. They build systems. They consistently take the steps that, in time, will ensure they reach their ultimate goal.

They don't wish. They don't hope.

They just *do* what their plan says, consistently and without fail.

---

*"Arnold Schwarzenegger's BluePrint To Cut: Vision," Bodybuilding.com, September 6, 2016, www.bodybuilding.com/fun/arnold-schwarzeneggers-blueprint-to-cut-vision.html.

They forget the goal and focus solely on the process. (We'll talk a lot—and I do mean a lot—about processes later on.)

And Definitely Don't Worry About Smart Goals

The main point of this chapter is to debunk the idea that maintaining a laser focus on your end goal is both motivating and a requirement for eventual success.

But there's another goal-setting premise that also gets in your way, especially if you're trying to accomplish a major goal. Conventional wisdom—and a boatload of books and articles—say we should establish "SMART" goals: Every goal should be specific, meaningful, attainable, realistic, and time bound.

I'm cool with "specific." Every goal should be specific. How will you know you've arrived if you never knew where you were going? And how will you follow the right process to get there?

"Meaningful" is a problem. No goal can be *made* meaningful. A goal either has meaning or it doesn't. The more you work to find or contrive or manufacture some sense of meaning, the less likely you are to achieve the goal.

It's impossible to "find" the meaning in a particular goal. While sometimes it does happen—if you're really lucky—that a meaningful goal finds you, most of the time the meaning in a goal is the result of immersing yourself in a routine and a set of tasks. Just as you gain motivation from small, repeated successes, you also find meaning in those successes.

"Time bound" is also a problem. Setting a date for completion is important, but it in no way helps you focus. Most goals tend to make an already complicated life even more complicated. Think about the last time you wrote a list of business or personal goals. When you finished, did you think, "Wow, this is awesome because I have a clear direction and purpose," or did you think, "Oh crap, how will I ever get all this done"?

I'm guessing you thought the latter—if not right away, certainly after a day or two.

"Attainable" is also a problem. There's nothing inspiring about an attainable goal. Attainable goals are targets, not goals. "I will cold-call twenty prospects today" is a target; just pick up the phone twenty times and you meet the target. That may be an important goal if it helps you meet your sales quotas, but it's far from inspirational.

Think of it this way: Your boss tells you to finish a report by noon. That's specific, meaningful (well, kind of), attainable, and time bound; your boss has provided most of the "important" aspects of a "great goal." But anything your boss asks you to do is a task, not a goal.

Only you can set a goal.

And then, only you can forget about that goal.

Successful People Forget About the Goal

If you've ever felt overwhelmed by a huge physical task and broken it down into small parts, you know it works. Maybe you were hiking and realized you had three miles to go before you reached the summit, and you decided to just focus on making it to the next turn on the trail, and then the next, and then the next. In essence, you forgot about the goal and broke it down into smaller steps.

Or maybe you were painting your house and realized you had seven rooms to go, and you decided to just focus on painting this wall, then the next wall . . .

Or maybe you had to create a seventy-page sales proposal and decided to just focus on completing one section at a time and then work on the next section. In each case the distance from here to there seemed so great that you decided to forget about the end goal and just focus on the process.

It worked.

And it will work again.

What should you do? It's easy:

Dream big.

Set a huge goal.

Commit to your huge goal.

Create a process that ensures you can reach your goal.

Then forget about your huge goal and work your process instead.

Make this your mantra where goals are concerned: "I will set it . . . and then I will *forget* it."

Take my example of the marathon, a goal that appears on thousands of bucket lists. To actually run a marathon, you will someday need to run a little over twenty-six miles—but if you're just starting out, you don't need to run that far today. Once you set your goal, create a process that will help you reach that goal. (Remember, the main purpose of a goal is to establish the right process and routine to achieve that goal.)

Say you aren't in particularly good shape, so your process calls for you to run one mile on the first day. While today you can't run a marathon, you can run one mile.

And because running that mile today is all you need to accomplish, you automatically feel good about yourself. You did exactly what you set out to do—and that motivates you to run again tomorrow.

At some point your process might require you to run 1.5 miles. Will running farther be more difficult? Sure, but you can do it. (If you've run a mile a day for a couple of weeks, trust me: You will be able to run 1.5 miles.) And after you do, you will naturally feel good about yourself all over again.

Plus, compared with where you started, you've already improved—and improvement feels awesome too.

Compared with running 26 miles, being able to run only 1.5 miles feels anything but awesome. But who cares? Right now you aren't focused on 26 miles. You don't have to get to *there*. You have to care only about today.

Because of that, your huge goal is no longer important. Your *process* is important—and where your process is concerned, you're a success.

On certain days during the following week you may have to run farther. Or you may not; what you need to do depends on the routine you have established. Either way, what matters is not how you currently compare with your eventual goal. What matters is that you consistently work your process and do what you set out to do, each and every day.

If you dedicate yourself to working your process, you will make progress. Success is inevitable.

And one day you'll wake up and realize you can run five miles . . . and then ten . . . and then twenty . . . because each day you compared yourself with what you needed to achieve *that day* instead of with what you needed to achieve *someday*.

Follow your process and someday you will run that marathon. You will have gone from here to there—almost without thinking about there.

And somehow, almost magically, you will have stayed motivated and enthusiastic.

How did that happen?

Forgetting Your Goal Unleashes the Power of Feedback (and Motivation)

Two essential truths:

> None of us receives enough positive feedback.
>
> Each of us is our own worst critic.

Feedback is based primarily on some form of comparison. If your boss says, "You did a great job," an implicit comparison is at play: Compared with a standard, spoken or unspoken, you performed relatively well. (Not relatively as in "somewhat" but relatively as in "compared with a standard.")

The same is true when you give yourself feedback. In effect, you compare what you just did with what you expect of yourself. But you will never be happy with what you see if you're measuring yourself against your eventual goal. You won't stack up. You *can't* stack up.

And you will feel terrible about yourself.

Focus on the process, though, and every day that you stick to your routine you will feel good about yourself.

For example:

- If you planned to eat three healthy meals today, and you did eat three healthy meals . . . awesome! You deserve to feel great—and that sense of fulfillment will motivate you to take the long walk you plan for tomorrow.

- If you planned to save $200 this month, and you did save $200 . . . awesome! You deserve to pat yourself on the back—and that feeling of accomplishment will motivate you to save the $220 you plan to save next month.
- If you planned to finish one class this semester, and you not only did so but also got an A in the class . . . double awesome! You deserve to feel proud—and your success will motivate you to complete the two classes you plan to take next semester.

Lose forty pounds? Forget it, at least for now. Save a million dollars? Forget it, at least for now. Earn a bachelor's degree? Forget it, at least for now.

Those are your goals. You set them, but for now you must forget them, because you will never be able to give yourself positive feedback when you constantly compare yourself with your end goal.

You will always be your worst critic because by definition you will never measure up.

And in time you will give up. The work will be too hard and the rewards too few.

That's why you need to forget the goal. What matters is the process.

If your process is one designed to get you where you

eventually want to go, all you have to do is work your process—and sticking with your process is so much easier when you create that self-reinforcing feedback loop of Success → Motivation → More Success → More Motivation → More Success.

That's the way I got one of my huge goals to actually love me back.

HOW I GOT MORE THAN JUST MY MOM TO READ MY *INC.* POSTS

If the first rule of Fight Club is "You do not talk about Fight Club," the first rule of ghostwriting is "You do not talk about your clients."

In my case that's certainly true; I sign nondisclosure agreements so restrictive my firstborn child may as well be pledged as surety. That's the nature of the business, but it's challenging to market yourself when you can't talk about the great projects you've completed or the notable clients you've worked for.

So I started writing for Inc.com in order to have published work appearing in my name on a highly reputable platform. That way potential clients may read it and think, "I really liked that . . . and hey, he's a ghostwriter. I need a ghostwriter."

Then I realized I could get paid for writing for *Inc.* If I committed to publishing a certain number of posts a month, they would pay me a flat fee for each post. It wasn't a lot, but because I was willing to write for free (I saw "free advertising" as the pro quo for that particular quid) any money I earned would be gravy.

Then I realized I could get paid a lot for writing for *Inc.*—as long as I was incredibly successful. Instead of being paid on a per-post basis, I could be paid by number of page views generated; the more views, the more I would make.

Keep in mind each view was worth only 0.0095 cents; in other words, I would earn $9.50 per thousand views. To make serious money I would have to generate serious views. Monthly compensation was capped at $10,000, which translated to 1,050,000 views, and to date no one had ever "capped out."

The more I thought about it, the less it made sense for me to choose to be paid by the post. Taking a flat fee was the conservative approach and would limit my potential compensation. Why not bet on myself?

So that became my huge goal: generate 1,050,000 page views a month.

Even though I was starting at zero.

I had limited success early on. For the first few weeks most of my posts did fewer than a thousand page views. Depressing? Yeah. The distance from *here,* a handful of page views, to *there,* over a million page views, seemed impossible to cross.

So I forgot about my huge goal. I focused on what I could control: what I did every day. After a little experimentation and a lot of thought, I settled on a process.

Because the Internet never sleeps, here's what I did every day:

1. **Write a new post.** Without fail. No excuses.
2. **Build relationships.** I contacted three people who tweeted my posts that day, choosing the three who seemed most influential, the most noteworthy, the most "something" (even if that "something" was just "thoughtful comment"). Then I sent an e-mail—not a tweet—and said thanks. My goal was to make a genuine connection.
3. **Build my network.** I contacted one person who might be a great source for a future post. I aimed high: CEOs, founders, entrepreneur-celebrities . . . people with instant credibility and engaged followings. Many didn't respond. But some did. And some have become friends and appear in this book.
4. **Add three more items to my "list of great headlines."** Headlines make or break posts: A great post with a terrible headline will not get read. So I worked hard to learn what worked for other people—and to adapt their techniques for my own use.
5. **Evaluate recent results.** I looked at page views. I looked at shares and likes and tweets. I tried to figure out what readers responded to, what readers cared about. Writing for a big audience has little to do with pleasing yourself and everything to do with pleasing an audience, and the only way to know what worked was to know the audience.
6. **Ignore my editor.** I liked my editor. But I didn't want her input because she knew only what worked for columnists who were read by a maximum of 300,000 people each

55

month. My goal was to triple that, which meant I needed to do things differently. We occasionally disagreed, and early on I lost some of those battles. Once my numbers started to climb, I won a lot more often, until eventually I was able to do my own thing.

Sounds simple, right? In a way it was, because I followed a self-reinforcing process:

- Posting frequently allowed me to improve my skills more quickly, increase my chances of writing "home run" posts that would go viral, and—not incidentally—build a library of posts for new readers to someday discover.
- Building connections provided an ever-expanding list of great content sources.
- Experimenting frequently with headlines allowed me to quickly learn to craft better headlines, and eventually I developed my own style (which was widely copied, so I've had to constantly adapt, but that's okay).
- The more I posted and connected and experimented, the more data points I could evaluate and the better I could understand what readers responded to, which led to more and more people reading my posts.

How many more? The first month I did just over 35,000 page views. (Ugh—but I kept my head down and stuck with the process.) The next month I did nearly 100,000. (Cool.) The next month I did over 300,000. (Very cool.) The next month I did nearly 900,000 page views. (Very, very cool.)

The fifth month one of my posts was the most shared post on LinkedIn . . . and that month I did 2.1 million page views. (And for the last couple of years I've averaged over 1.5 million views a month.)

From a day-to-day point of view, nothing had changed: I still followed the same process.

But what had changed was my results and, to some extent, me. Following my process had helped me develop the skills, the strategies, and, just as important, the confidence and perseverance required to reach my huge goal.

Still, you may be thinking, "Okay, getting lots of page views is impressive—but is that really a huge goal?"

Maybe not. In a moment we'll look at how one person used the power of process to reach a once-in-a-generation achievement.

But first let's look at how you can accomplish a goal that isn't practical or numbers based—but one that most of us definitely hope to achieve: being more likable.

BELIEVE IT OR NOT, THERE *IS* A PROCESS FOR BUILDING GREAT RELATIONSHIPS

No one has enough friends. (I definitely don't.)

And if that's not reason enough to be likable, we tend to do business and build professional relationships with people we like. We're instinctively drawn to people who are modest, agreeable, polite, kind . . . in short, to people who are genuinely likable.

So hey, if you don't want to be more likable just for the sake of building more and better relationships, it's also good business, you type-A, nose-to-the-grindstone, ladder-climbing high achiever, you.

But how do people decide whether they like you, especially once they've gotten to know you a little better?

The answer often lies in what likable people *don't* do.

So here's a checklist. The next time you're heading out to a social gathering or networking event or any situation where you'll interact with people in a relatively casual setting, review this list. See it as your checklist of things not to do.

Again, the key isn't to think, "I want people to like me." That is your goal, but forget about your goal and just follow the process.

1. Don't talk a lot.

I know that sounds odd, because friendly people tend to be gregarious and outgoing. And there's certainly nothing wrong with that—but there's a big difference between friendly and likable.

Likable people already know what they know. They want to

know what other people know. They ask questions. They ask for details. They care about what other people think, and they show it by listening.

That makes the people they meet feel important. It makes the people they meet feel likable. (As well they should, because they are.)

And it makes the people they meet like them for making them feel that way.

2. Don't blame.

Friends make mistakes. Employees don't meet expectations. Vendors don't deliver on time. It's easy to blame other people for our problems.

But we are also to blame. Maybe we didn't provide enough training. Maybe we didn't build in enough of a buffer. Maybe we asked for too much too soon.

Taking responsibility when things go wrong instead of blaming others isn't masochistic; it's empowering—because then we focus on doing things better, or smarter, the next time.

And when we get better or smarter, we're also more likable.

As long as we also . . .

3. Don't try to impress.

No one likes us for our clothes, our cars, our possessions, our titles, or our accomplishments. Those are all "things." People may like our things—but that doesn't mean they like us.

Sure, superficially they might seem to, but superficial is also insubstantial, and a relationship that is not based on substance is not a real relationship.

The only way to form genuine relationships is to stop trying to impress . . . and start being yourself.

4. Don't interrupt.

Interrupting isn't just rude. When we interrupt someone, what we're really saying is "I'm listening to you not so I can understand what you're saying; I'm listening to you so I can decide what *I* want to say."

Want people to like you? Listen to what *they* say. Focus on what *they* say. Ask questions to make sure you understand what *they* say.

They'll love you for it—and you'll love how that makes you feel.

5. Don't control.

At work, you may be the boss. You may be in charge. The buck may stop with you.

Everywhere else, the only thing you really control is you. People who try to control other people—tell them what they should do, what they should think, what they should feel—have decided that their goals, their dreams, or even just their opinions are more important than everyone else's.

People like people who help. Don't tell someone else what to do. Ask them how you can help them do what they want to do.

They won't just like you for it. They'll love you for it.

6. Don't preach.

People who criticize also tend to preach. And judge.

The higher you rise and the more you accomplish, the more likely you are to think you know everything—and to tell people everything you think you know.

When you speak with more finality than foundation, people may hear you—but they don't listen.

Want to be instantly likable? Be the person who has accomplished very cool things . . . but manages to make other people feel like they are the ones who have accomplished very cool things.

7. Don't dwell on the past.

The past is valuable. We should all learn from our mistakes.

And then we should let our mistakes go.

Easier said than done? It depends on your focus. When something bad happens to you, see that as a chance to learn something you didn't know. When another person makes a mistake, see that as an opportunity to be kind, forgiving, and understanding.

The past is just training; it doesn't define you. Think about what went wrong, but only in terms of how you will make sure that next time you will get it right.

Optimism—rational, reasoned, justifiable optimism—is contagious.

And very, very likable.

Try it. If you want to make new friends, or to make better friends, don't focus on that goal. Focus on following the process above. You'll meet more people and have conversations that are more substantive than superficial. You'll give more people a chance to share who they really are . . . which gives you the chance to decide whether they are someone you want to play a bigger part in your life.

On the flip side, you will instantly be more likable, which will attract people to you. And ultimately you will build better relationships because the process ensures your attention is placed on other people, not on yourself.

Your goal—building more and better relationships—won't get you there. Becoming more likable will get you there.

Process will get you there.

Even if you want to accomplish something almost unimaginable.

THE POWER OF FORGETTING A HUGE GOAL: HOW JERRY SEINFELD BECAME *THE* JERRY SEINFELD

Imagine you want to be a comedian. That means you need material—lots and lots of material. You can't perform the same act year after year. You constantly need new jokes, new insights, new stories.

(In much the same way that Domino's isn't in the pizza business, it's in the delivery business, comedians aren't really in the performing business—they're in the writing business. If Domino's can't deliver consistently, its pizzas are irrelevant. If comedians can't write consistently, their performing is irrelevant.)

Now imagine you're a young Jerry Seinfeld. And imagine that, although you never say it out loud, you dream of being a comedian. And somehow you realize that the way to be a better comic is to write better jokes . . . and that the only way to write better jokes is to write every day.

Wait for inspiration? Nope. Wait for lightning to strike? Nope. Waiting accomplishes nothing. You need to write each and every day.

So you get a large wall calendar, one that shows the entire year. You hang it in a place you can't miss it. And every day, once you've accomplished your task—remember, your task isn't to become a great comedian, your task is to write new material—you put a red *X* over that date.

"After a few days," Seinfeld told Brad Isaac, "you'll have a chain. Just keep at it and the chain will grow longer every day. You'll like seeing that chain, especially when you get a few weeks under your belt. Your only job is to not break the chain."*

Your only job is to not break the chain.

Seinfeld didn't focus on his ultimate goal. He didn't focus on becoming a headlining comedian. He didn't focus on developing an iconic hit TV series. He didn't focus on earning, according to *Forbes,* $267 million in one year.

Want to be your own version of Jerry Seinfeld? Keep checking off those boxes. Within a few days you'll start to embrace those small successes. Within a few weeks you won't be able to imagine doing things differently.

And one day you'll look up and realize that *here* has gotten a lot closer to *there* than you ever imagined possible.

If you follow the right process, that is.

---

*Gina Trapani, "Jerry Seinfeld's Productivity Secret," Lifehacker, July 24, 2007, https://lifehacker.com/281626/jerry-seinfelds-productivity-secret.

CHAPTER 3

Your Goal Must Always
Choose Your Process

Later in this book I'll lay out strategies to enjoy, sometimes even love, the things you need to do to succeed. (It's amazing how your perspective will change when you see results.)

For now, though, let's start with what you *need* to do in order to succeed.

Let's use our example of walking the Appalachian Trail. Create a plan to walk twelve miles a day, stick to that plan . . . and 180-odd days later you will achieve your goal.

Or let's say you want to lose forty pounds. Create a plan to consume three hundred fewer calories than you burn every day, stick to that plan . . . and 466 days later you will achieve your goal. (Focusing on the forty pounds, or the 466 days it takes to lose them, is a perfect example of how horrifyingly huge a goal can be when you're just getting started.)

Let's say you want to write a book. Create a plan to write a thousand words a day, stick to that plan . . . and seventy to eighty days later (depending on how long-winded you are) you will achieve your goal.

How do you think I wrote this book? If I had started every day by thinking, "I need to write a book," I would have quit early on. Instead I started each day knowing, for example, that "today I will write the section on how not sharing your goals with other people can actually make you more likely to succeed." I didn't worry about the total word count. I used the Seinfeld technique. My goal was to channel my inner Fleetwood Mac and never break the chain. I worried only about what I needed to do each day.

That's why, where your process is concerned, you don't get to choose what you *want* to do. You get to choose your goal—but after that, what you want to do is irrelevant. What matters is *what you need to do to achieve your goal*. You can't have dessert with every meal and lose weight. (Well, theoretically you can . . . but jeez, that will be hard.) You can't complete a triathlon without doing an awful lot of running, biking, and swimming. (Well, theoretically you can . . . as long as they give you a week to complete the race.) You can't get promoted without outworking everyone around you. (Well, theoretically you can . . . but don't you want to earn the job instead of politicking your way in?)

So don't start unless you're truly willing to pay the price.

HOW TO CREATE A SUCCESSFUL PROCESS

You might be tempted to skip this section. Don't. Process is everything.

And maybe just as important, creating a successful process is hugely motivating in and of itself. By the time you've mapped out your process, you'll be incredibly motivated to get started. If you struggle with procrastination, the boost of motivation you will feel from successfully creating a successful process (I know that sounds cheesy, but it's true) will leave you itching to get started.

Seriously. Try it. Then tell me I'm wrong.

That's what successes, no matter how small, do for you.

Now, here are the steps for creating a successful process:

1. Set your goal.

To make it easy, let's say you've decided to run a marathon. (I use the word "easy" because it's challenging to design a routine to develop a niche skill. Fortunately, for this goal training plans are easy to come by. Google "train for a marathon" and you'll instantly get dozens of results: some for beginners, some for intermediate runners, etc.)

2. Set aside decision anxiety and choose a reasonably promising routine.

For now, just pick a process that matches your current fitness level. Don't worry about which training program is "best," especially because you have no way of knowing which program is best for you. (In this case, looking for the "best" not only is a time-wasting rabbit hole but also automatically ensures you'll begin to second-guess the plan you picked the instant your training gets difficult.)

So just pick a plan, trusting that any plan that ranks highly in search results found its way there for a reason.

Then . . .

3. If necessary, customize your process to be extremely specific.

Writing "Go jogging three days this week" on a Post-it doesn't mean you have a process. What does "go jogging" mean? And which days will you run? How far? How fast?

Instead of "go jogging," here's what your process should look like:

Monday: Run 1.5 miles.

Tuesday: Stretch (list the different stretches) for 20 minutes.

Wednesday: Run 2 miles.

Thursday: Walk at a pace of three miles per hour for 45 minutes.

Friday: . . .

A good process tells you precisely what you need to accomplish at every step along the way. That way you know exactly what to do, and you know when you have actually accomplished what you need to do.

Say your goal is to increase your client base. "Cold-call three prospects" is a specific, actionable plan. If your goal is to get promoted, "volunteer for a cross-departmental improvement team" is a specific, actionable plan. If you're seeking a degree, "study for two hours and take a practice test" is a specific, actionable plan.

Setting a clear and specific target for each day's effort automatically supports feedback: Either you did what you planned to do (great!) or you didn't (boo!).

4. Rework your schedule.

Training for a marathon involves a significant amount of running, especially as you get in better shape and build the strength and endurance needed to achieve your goal. Plus, you may need to perform strength and flexibility exercises on a regular basis.

All your training will naturally take time, and freeing up that time means changing your current routine.

Maybe you'll stop lifting weights. Maybe you'll start getting up earlier. Maybe you'll decide you can no longer keep up with the Kardashians. No matter what, some things—maybe a lot of things—will have to change. (I reworked my entire daily, weekly, and monthly schedules—writing, speaking, consulting, exercise, family time, you name it—in order to write this book. Lots of things had to change. How could they not?)

Look at the process you created and determine what changes you need to make to your current daily routine so you can reliably work that process.

If you don't, you will never succeed.

5. Map out your daily plan.

This is the easy part. Just take the training plan you found and put it on a calendar.

For example, your first week might look like this:

Sunday: 30-minute walk

Monday: rest

Tuesday: 1.5-mile run

Wednesday: 3-mile run

Thursday: 1.5-mile run

Friday: rest

Saturday: 3-mile run

Then sense-check your plan against your new daily routine to make sure it works.

6. Work the process.

Maybe that first three-mile run was too hard and you had to walk some portion of it. That's okay; just make sure you complete the three miles.

More important, don't compare yourself with other people. Don't worry about whether you're as fast as your neighbor; you probably won't be. Don't worry about whether you're as fit as you were in high school; you *definitely* won't be. The only thing that matters is that you can check off the box beside each day's activity.

That's the only "comparison" you care about.

And when you do check off each box, take a second to congratulate yourself. At this point, consistently working the plan is the only performance standard that matters.

But just because you set specific goals doesn't mean you should murder anyone to see them through. If you plan to run three miles and halfway into the run you feel a twinge in your hamstring, don't push through the pain. Cut your run short. While you didn't run three miles, you did go for your run—and you haven't risked injuring yourself.

Even though there will always be small setbacks, as long as you don't miss your scheduled runs, you will get in better shape over the long term. So if you do feel that twinge and let discretion be the better part of valor, you get to feel twice as good about yourself: You didn't miss your workout and you made a smart short-term decision that supports your long-term goal.

Win-win!

7. Fix your schedule problems.

No matter how hard you tried to predict the future, your reworked schedule probably didn't always work in practice. Trading off a few household responsibilities may not have worked. Leaving work early to get to the gym may not have always worked.

Something won't work, and when that happens, what usually gives first? Your new process.

Instead of giving up, fix whatever schedule problems have arisen. There is always a way.

Just keep in mind that sometimes you may have to go for a run at 11:00 p.m. or bring work home or get up early to finish that project . . . because you don't miss workouts, and you don't let coworkers down, and you don't let opportunities slip away. (More on that in a moment.)

8. *Your results may vary, so adapt accordingly.*

But don't make changes to your process because you're tired or lazy or bored—make changes because those changes increase your likelihood of ultimate success.

For example, most people need greater time to recover from exercise as they age; our bodies don't recover as quickly from high-intensity or long-duration workouts. So when I was training to ride a Gran Fondo, my initial plan—created by Jeremiah Bishop, a world-class cyclist and a guy I definitely wasn't going to argue with—specified three rest days each week.

After a month we decided to experiment: I rode six days a week for several weeks. To our surprise, my endurance and speed increased more quickly than under the original plan. (Now I know why: According to tests I've taken, my capacity to recover from exercise is relatively high.)

Ultimately, recovery is specific to the individual. Just as people respond to physical or psychological stress differently, athletes respond differently to different recovery strategies.

I do better with less rest; other people do better with more.

But I didn't know that when I started. I *couldn't* know that when I started.

And neither can you.

Always wait until you can evaluate real results before you modify your process. Don't assume you somehow know better— let the data *show* you what is better.

If you're paying attention, it will.

Want another example? In the next section we'll look at one that millions of people can relate to—and, I hope, benefit from.

But keep in mind that the following is just an example. Maybe you aren't trying to lose weight. That's okay; what I lay out is a daily checklist. For some people, weekly schedules work best. That way they can adapt and adjust—slightly—as necessary in order to stay on track. For others, a daily checklist works best: They want to know exactly what they will do now, then next, then next. Following a daily checklist is the best way to stay perfectly on track. Which is right for you?

If you're new to the process of following a process, use a daily checklist. That way, each time you tick off a box you get that immediate rush of feedback from success—and you'll be excited about ticking off the next box.

WANT TO LOSE TEN POUNDS IN THIRTY DAYS? YOU CAN!

Get two thousand people in a room and at least half will say they'd like to lose a little weight. Get two thousand hard-charging, go-getting, type-A personalities in a room and many of them will say they'd like to lose weight fast.

So while I was surprised, I probably shouldn't have been.

The organizer of the business conference had hustled over

right before I went onstage. The speaker scheduled to appear after me couldn't make it because his flight had been delayed.

"Can you go another forty-five minutes to fill the time?" he asked. "Maybe do a Q&A?"

I'm not a huge fan of mass question-and-answer sessions because many questions tend to be hyperspecific to the individual and the answers therefore totally boring to the group. So I finished my presentation and asked the audience to suggest topics. The A/V guy posted their submissions on the giant screen behind me, and I had the audience vote by applause for their favorite topic.

Which subject won? Not raising capital. Not finding investors. Not leading better, or hiring smarter, or harnessing the creative power of employees.

Nope. This was the overwhelming favorite: "How can I lose ten pounds in one month?"

As I said, maybe I shouldn't have been surprised. Millions of people have tried and failed to lose weight.

Before we start: I'm not a nutritionist. I'm not a certified exercise professional. I have no official credentials. Yet I know that the following works, because in less than a month I went from 172 to 161 pounds.

Here's what I shared:

My success was not based solely on the program or its details. I didn't come up with a trendy new diet, didn't find some magic way to "trick" my body into losing weight, didn't find some groundbreaking new strategy that made weight loss effortless . . . because all that stuff is just feel-good happy horse-shit. (Yep, I'm a southern boy.) My success was based on creating a process I knew would allow me to achieve my goal *as long as I followed that process.*

I didn't wish. I didn't hope. I didn't look for the easy way. (The easy way never works.) I built an effective plan, and once I did, success was inevitable. All I had to do was stick to the plan.

I set it, I used it to inform my process, and then I forgot it and focused each day solely on what I had to do that day in order to work the plan.

Here goes.

1. Start with a fast day.

I'm normally not a fast/cleanse kind of guy, but drinking only clear liquids for twenty-four hours is a great way to hit the reset button on your normal habits. I combined my start day with a scheduled colonoscopy; hey, why not double-dip? (Wait—that didn't sound so great.) Plus, some experts claim that an occasional fast is good for you.

Best of all, your stomach will shrink, and when you do start eating again, you'll feel full more quickly and therefore will eat less.

Just stop eating at, oh, 8:00 p.m. tonight, drink only clear liquids tomorrow, and start back up with a healthy breakfast the following day.

Think you can't go a day without eating? You can. It's not that hard. And you'll probably lose a pound in the process, which gets you off to a nice mental start.

2. Exercise first thing every morning.

Yes, Saturdays and Sundays too. But you don't have to exercise for long. Twenty minutes of moderate cardio is enough.

You'll get your day off to a great start, you'll be less likely to overeat later (because you'll know overeating means you wasted some of the effort you put in), and studies show that twenty minutes of exercise improves your mood for up to twelve hours. Win-win-win!

3. Eat four almonds fifteen minutes before every meal.

I'm sure there's science behind this, but here's what I know: I'm always less hungry and therefore eat less when I have four almonds fifteen minutes before a meal.

Plus, a little healthy fat is good for you.

4. Drink a glass of water right before every meal.

One, drinking more water is good for you. Two, you'll partly fill your stomach and will feel full faster.

5. Always stop eating the moment you start to feel full.

We tend to eat for taste, which means we eat past the point of feeling full—and that's one reason we put on weight. Pay attention to your body's signals and stop eating as soon as it's telling you you're full.

When you eat too quickly, that "full" signal will reach your brain after you're actually full. To help the process along, eat slower than you normally do.

In a few days your stomach will adapt to the new reality, any hunger pangs you feel early on will fade, and you'll reset your perception of "full."

6. Don't eat anything white.

White flours and white sugars are the enemy. That means that foods like white breads, cookies, white pasta, white rice, and white potatoes are out. (The same is true for "white fats" like butter and full-fat cheese.)

Then just replace the white stuff with vegetables, fruits, and lean proteins.

You'll lose a couple pounds (at least) just from taking this one step.

7. Make sure every meal is healthy.

Easier said than done, right? Nope. Easily done. Just include a serving of lean protein (fish, poultry, egg whites, etc.) with two servings of vegetables or one serving each of vegetables and fruit.

Will that require a little planning? Of course it will. So every day map out what you will eat the next day, and buy and even prepare your food ahead of time if possible. Then when it's time to eat, you won't have to make any decisions about what to eat— you'll just eat what you planned.

Remember, decisions are behavioral change killers, so eliminate as many decisions as possible.

And notice you aren't counting calories; I didn't. If you eat healthy meals and don't add a lot of butter, dressings, toppings, etc., the calories basically take care of themselves. Besides, you already know the foods you shouldn't eat; you don't need a calorie app to tell you.

8. Toss in a snack.

Eating less at every meal—and eliminating white foods—will leave you hungry at odd times of the day. I ate a protein bar for a midafternoon snack: simple, convenient, and easy to eat on the go.

Remember, snacking with a purpose is smart. Snacking just to snack is not.

9. Burn about five hundred extra calories a day.

Note that I said "extra." If you already work out, then those calories are already factored into your daily routine and result in your current weight. So you'll need to burn more calories.

How? That's up to you. But keep in mind that, unless you're a high-intensity-workout fool, you'll need to work out for at least an hour to burn five hundred calories. (Walking at a brisk 3.5 miles per hour burns only three hundred to four hundred calories an hour, depending on your weight.)

Cycling is my favorite exercise for burning calories: If I average between sixteen and eighteen miles per hour and toss in some decent hills, I can easily burn seven hundred to eight hundred calories an hour.

What you do is up to you . . . but you need to do whatever you decide to do. Burning an extra five hundred calories a day—as long as you don't increase your calorie intake—will strip off about four pounds by the end of the month and you'll be less likely to overeat at mealtimes because you won't want to spoil the hard work you put in.

There are plenty of exercise calculators you can use. Pick one, pick some activities, and get to work.

10. Cheat wisely.

Like sweets? Me too. But sweets are all about taste, and taste can be quickly satisfied. I let three or four chocolate chips melt in my mouth, one at a time, after some of my meals.

The calories were negligible but the taste was nice . . . and I felt a little less like a food monk.

11. Keep a food journal.

The Hawthorne effect works: When we know we are being observed, we instinctively change our behaviors. In this case, of course, you will be the one doing the observing.

Plus, writing down everything you eat will keep you from doing any "mindless" eating and will keep you from underestimating—because we all underestimate—what you actually consume.

So write everything down. Then total up your calories at the end of the day. Ideally, you'll eat four hundred to five hundred fewer calories than you did before you started, and at the end of the month that will be worth four pounds or so.

12. Check off each step in the process.

Notice I said "process," not "progress." The key is not to focus on your goal; the key is to focus on following your process. So make yourself a chart and check off each time you follow the process:

Early-morning exercise: check.

Almonds before meals: check.

Glass of water before meals: check.

Stop when full: check.

No white foods: check.

Every meal healthy: check.

Smart snack: check.

Burn five hundred extra calories: check.

Cheat wisely: check.

What if you miss a check or two?

It's not the end of the world—but it is reason to adjust your daily routine to ensure that tomorrow you can check off every box. I quickly realized I needed to prepare all my meals the night before so I was never caught short. I also bought a box of protein bars and a bag of almonds to put in my backpack so I would never be without.

And because my schedule, like yours, was often unpredictable, I realized the only way I could be absolutely sure to exercise every day was to get up early and do it first thing. I used the twenty-minute cardio period as a warm-up and then rode my bike or jogged afterward. While it wasn't fun to get up early, it was fun to always complete that task.

I got to feel good about myself every day for completing all the other tasks and, at the end of each day, for knowing that I had followed my process and achieved everything I had set out to achieve that day.

Lose ten pounds in a month? After a few days it didn't sound like such a huge hurdle. I knew as long as I put in the work, I would make it. Every day put me one step closer. All I had to do was work the plan and success was inevitable.

Inevitable success is the best success of all—and it will happen when you set your goal, forget your goal, and focus on working your process.

As long as, of course, the process you create will realistically help you achieve your goal. It's easy to get swept up in a dream and ignore the fact that your approach must be realistic.

For example, let's say you want to become a multimillionaire.

WANT TO GET RICH? YOU CAN!

Completing all the steps required to run a marathon takes months. Completing all the steps to lose ten pounds in thirty days takes, well, thirty days.

Building exceptional wealth? That takes years. Getting rich—however you define "rich"—is an incredibly ambitious goal.

Call it a life goal.

How do you achieve a lifelong objective? Let's say your target is, oh, $50 million. Totally unrealistic?

Nope. The goal isn't unrealistic. Genetics don't play a part. Experience, education, and connections are all important but not required. Tens of thousands of people from all walks of life achieve that level of wealth. The goal isn't unrealistic . . . but for the millions of people who hope to achieve significant wealth, the *approach* is what is unrealistic—and what ensures that they never come close.

Of course, money isn't everything. As John D. Rockefeller, America's first billionaire, said, "If your only goal is to become rich, you'll never achieve it." His point is well taken: If the only thing you care about is making money, no matter how much money you make, it will never be enough. Still, even though we each define and calculate success differently—as well we should—most of us would like wealth to factor into our equation somewhere.

The best way to determine the right process for achieving a

life goal is to study people who have actually achieved that goal. (Why reinvent the wheel?) Start at the end and work backward.

In this case we'll use *Top 400 Individual Tax Returns Reporting the Largest Adjusted Gross Incomes,* a report the IRS issues on an irregular basis. Reading the report is as exciting as the title sounds—the IRS Statistics of Income division is evidently where fun goes to die—but if you want to get rich, there is some interesting data buried in all the charts and tables.

As of this writing, the latest report I could find was for 2009, which to you and me seems like a long time ago but to the government clearly seems up to date.

In 2009 it took $77.4 million in adjusted gross income to make the top four hundred. And that amount only just let you crack the list. The average earnings on the list were $202.4 million.

Where it gets interesting is *how* the top four hundred made their money:

- Wages and salaries: 8.6 percent
- Interest: 6.6 percent
- Dividends: 13 percent
- Partnerships and corporations: 19.9 percent
- Capital gains: 45.8 percent

The top four hundred averaged $92.6 million in capital gains. That's 16 percent of the total capital gains reported by *all* taxpayers. (Do the math and the whole one-percenter thing that was popular a few years ago sounds like an overestimate.)

Obvious conclusions:

- Working for a salary won't make you rich.
- Neither will making only safe "income" investments.
- Neither will investing only in large companies.
- Owning a business or businesses, even in part or partnership, not only could build a solid wealth foundation but could someday generate a huge financial windfall.

The data clearly supports the last point. A total of over 3,800 taxpayers have made the top 400 since 1992, but only 27 percent appear more than once, and only 2 percent appear ten or more times.

But You Say You Don't Trust the IRS?

Fine. Check out the top ten people on the annual *Forbes* billionaires list.

Whom do you find? The usual suspects. Bill Gates. Warren Buffett. Larry Ellison. David and Charles Koch. A collection of Walmart Waltons. Sheldon Adelson (proving, as if you need proof, that no one wins in casinos but the casinos). All entrepreneurs. I worked my way down into the two hundreds, and when I still couldn't find an employee, I got bored and quit looking.

Clearly getting rich, in financial terms, is the result of investing in yourself and others, taking risks, doing hundreds of small things right . . . and then doing one or two big things really, really right.

HAPPIER AND WEALTHIER

Here's a funny thing. I've spoken to dozens of successful entrepreneurs and all of them do the same thing. When we talk about the financial side of being an entrepreneur—exit strategies, revenues, IPOs, the ever-popular "cashing out"—they're interested but far from animated. But when we talk about the life of an entrepreneur, when we talk about how it feels to be an entrepreneur, every one of them lights up. They enthuse about the challenges, the responsibility, the sense of mission, the sense of purpose, the sense of fulfillment and excitement of working with and for a real team, the amazing feeling of empowerment and control over their own destinies.

It happens every time.

The bootstrappers, the ones with infinite dreams but, at least for the moment, negligible revenues, light up.

The successful entrepreneurs—like Joel Gascoigne, who helped expand Buffer from a personal project into a thriving business with a talented team, real revenues, and significant investment capital—light up.

The hugely successful entrepreneurs, like Scott Dorsey, who helped steer ExactTarget out of a garage, into an IPO, and then into an acquisition by Salesforce.com, light up. Dharmesh Shah, the cofounder of HubSpot, who took his vision of the future of marketing and turned it into a public company with a market capitalization of over $2 billion, lights up.

Every entrepreneur lights up when we talk about *being* an entrepreneur, because as entrepreneurs they feel alive. They feel free to chart their own courses, to make their own decisions, to make their own mistakes—to let the sky be the limit not just financially but also (and almost always more importantly) personally.

Hugely successful or barely off the ground, they haven't just started businesses. They've *become* something. They've become entrepreneurs.

And they already feel rich, regardless of income or wealth.

But if they hope to become wealthy in monetary terms, they are on the right track, because barring some stroke of financial lightning that no one could foresee, there is no way to accumulate millions of dollars in wealth unless you start your own business.

Maybe that business is selling a product or service. Maybe that business is day-trading. Maybe that business is becoming an actor or musician or entertainer or writer or any of a number of "professions" where you are in the business of you. (Actors get hired to play roles, so technically they work for someone else . . . but not really. Fundamentally actors—just like musicians and other entertainers—are in the business of *themselves*.)

The only way to become financially rich is to start your own business, even if it's just on the side. Even if it's just, at first, a slightly stepped-up hobby.

Any other approach will not make you rich.

If you want to amass significant wealth but you aren't willing to give up your current job—or spend your nights and weekends building a side business with considerable potential—your approach is the problem. Say your goal is to have $2 million in the bank. If you earn $50,000 a year in salary (a very nice wage), and you don't spend a penny of it and somehow manage not to pay any taxes either, it will still take forty years to save $2 million.

The goal isn't unrealistic. The approach—the process—is unrealistic.

Or say you want to amass tens of millions of dollars in wealth. If you aren't willing to work to create something new and different, if you aren't trying to do something Zuckerbergian, your goal isn't the problem. Your approach is the problem. If you aren't willing to find a new way to fill an ongoing and nearly universal need, if you aren't willing to do something Netflixian, your goal isn't the problem. Your approach is the problem.

You can't just open a corner restaurant and hope to become super wealthy. You can't stop there; you'll have to build a chain of restaurants. You can't just open a small boutique downtown. You can't stop there; you'll have to build an online clothing empire.

And if you think everything I've just written sounds depressing, that I'm crushing your dreams before you even start, you're wrong.

Everything I've just written is totally empowering. If you want to become wealthy, there *is* a way. If you want to achieve a huge goal, whatever your goal may be, there *is* a way.

Especially when you use the power of language to help you stay on track.

"I DON'T" ARE THE MAGIC WORDS FOR STAYING ON TRACK

I know what you're thinking: "Fine . . . but how will I ever stick with that process for a month when I always struggle to change my diet for one day?"

That's a good question. Changing your behavior—especially when doing something different basically means saying no to something you normally do—is really hard.

Most people trying to change their diet and exercise routine slowly chip away at their own resolve until they wind up doing something they didn't want to do . . . because they eventually couldn't say no to themselves.

That's one of the toughest parts of following a process, or creating a new habit, or simply trying something new and difficult: saying "no" to yourself. You want to take a day off and you can't say no to yourself. You want to have dessert and you can't say no to yourself. You want to run farther but you feel tired and you give in and don't say no to yourself.

And you end up doing what you didn't plan to do—or not doing what you planned to do.

So what is the best way to say no to yourself? It's easy: Stop saying "can't" and start saying "don't."

It works. Science says so. Researchers conducted a study: One group was given a simple temptation and told to say, in the face of that temptation, "I can't do (that)." The other group was told to say, "I don't do (that)."

What happened?

- Participants told to say "I can't" gave in to the temptation 61 percent of the time.
- Participants told to say "I don't" gave in to the temptation 36 percent of the time.

Pretty cool, right? It gets better.

The same researchers conducted a further experiment: Participants were told to set a personal long-term health and wellness goal. When their initial motivation flagged—as initial motivation inevitably does—one group was told to say, "I *can't* miss my workout." Another group was told to say, "I *don't* miss my workouts." (The control group was not given a temptation-avoidance strategy.)

Ten days later the researchers found:

- Three out of ten control group members stuck to their goal.
- One out of ten "I can't" group members stuck to their goal.
- Eight out of ten "I don't" group members stuck to their goal.

Not only was "I can't" less effective than "I don't"; "I can't" was less effective than using no strategy at all.

Why? According to the researchers, "The refusal frame 'I don't' is more persuasive than the refusal frame 'I can't' because the former connotes conviction to a higher degree. . . . Perceived conviction mediates the influence of refusal frame on persuasiveness."*

Or in language the rest of us understand, when we say "I can't," we give ourselves a way out. "I could, sure, but this time I'm choosing not to. You know, because I can't. Wait. Hmm. I probably shouldn't, but you know, maybe just this one time . . ."

Which of the following sound more powerful and affirmational?

- "I can't skip my workout today" or "I don't miss workouts"?
- "I can't give you a discount" or "We don't discount our products"?
- "I can't make time for that, so sorry" or "I don't have a single open slot in my calendar"?

"I can't" sounds tissue-paper thin because it's a decision based on external reasons or causes.

"I don't" sounds like a brick wall because it comes from deep inside you. It's part of your identity. It's who you are.

---

*Vanessa M. Patrick and Henrik Hagtvedt, "'I Don't' versus 'I Can't': When Empowered Refusal Motivates Goal-Directed Behavior," *Journal of Consumer Research,* 39, no. 2 (August 2012): 371–81, www.jstor.org/stable/10.1086/663212 ?seq=1#page_scan_tab_contents.

The power of "I don't" extends to both your mind-set and the impression you make on others.

1. YOU CAN'T MAKE EXCUSES TO YOURSELF.

Take "I don't miss workouts" or "I don't eat fast food."

When you "can't," you automatically start to find excuses, reasons why you can. When you "don't," you automatically start to find ways to ensure you do—because that is the person you have *become*.

That is the person you *are*.

Use the power of language to help turn what you want to be into who you are. Use the power of language to forge a new—and better—identity for yourself.

2. YOU COME ACROSS AS MORE CONFIDENT.

Take "We don't offer discounts."

Maybe you really don't want to offer discounts because your margins will suffer and competing on price is a slippery slope you can't afford. Instead of saying, weakly and apologetically, "I'm sorry, but we can't drop our prices any lower," say firmly and with conviction, "We don't offer discounts."

And then either remain silent and wait for a response or shift the conversation to what you *are* willing to do: provide a quicker turnaround or extend payment terms or break a large order down into smaller shipments.

Use "I don't" to ensure that what must be nonnegotiable remains nonnegotiable . . . and then shift to terms you are willing to negotiate.

3. YOU WON'T GET AS MUCH PUSHBACK ON YOUR RESOLUTIONS.

Take "I don't have time right now."

Say a friend of a friend says, "I'd love to work in your industry. Can we meet for coffee so I can get some advice?"

You'd love to say yes, but sometimes that's impossible. Saying, "I'm sorry, but I can't," inevitably results in the other person saying, "But I promise it will only take a minute and it would mean so much to me." And then you're trapped. You either consent to meet or decline and come across as rude.

Either way, you lose.

Instead say, "I'm sorry, but I don't have time in the next few weeks. Give me your card and maybe we can work something out down the road." Then you can say yes—if you decide to say yes—on your terms.

HERE'S A "DON'T" EVERYONE SHOULD SAY

"I don't care what other people think." Most of the time we should worry about what other people think . . . but not if it stands in the way of living the life we really want to live.

I can't care? The heck with that. I *don't* care.

You shouldn't care. It's your life, and there's only one option: Live it your way.

Of course, being confident and respected starts with deciding who you want to be . . . and that means choosing a goal to achieve. After all, we are not what we think or wish or dream—we are what we *do*.

Let's figure out what you want to do.

CHAPTER 4

Happiness Comes to Serial Achievers

Encouraging you to live your best life is easy.

Helping you decide what goals you should pursue—and achieve—in order to live that best life is a lot tougher. (Easy, now: I really like Oprah.)

That's why no one does it.

But I will.

Before I do, though, let's discuss a few other things.

HOW GOOD IS GOOD ENOUGH?

First, let's pretend Malcolm Gladwell is right and it takes approximately ten thousand hours of focused effort to become an expert in a challenging pursuit or field. (Actually, first let's pretend Malcolm Gladwell was the first to come up with the ten-thousand-hours premise.)

If Gladwell is basically right (and snarkiness aside, he always is—but I have better hair, so at least I've got that going for me), then the average person will need to put in about forty hours a week for five years to become highly accomplished in their chosen pursuit.

But most of us don't have forty hours a week to devote to accomplishing a huge goal unless it's career related—in which case, we typically spend a huge chunk of our time performing skills we've already learned instead of developing new skills that will lead us to greatness. We're more likely to become "superior" in that career pursuit, not world-class, not top 0.01 percent, but definitely more skilled than 95 percent of the population.

That's cool. You don't need to be a world-class athlete to (cliché alert) run a marathon, but if that is a goal you set, and you achieve that goal, you will then have accomplished something that 99.999 percent of the population never will. Because the average person can successfully train to run a marathon in less than a year . . . when you think of it that way, achieving the rank of "superior" is an excellent alternative to applying Gladwellian levels of effort.

Besides that, you don't want to try to become world-class in a variety of pursuits. It's incredibly difficult to perform at an extremely high level in very different—and sometimes conflicting—pursuits.

As Gladwell said on Lance Armstrong's *The Forward* podcast:

If you're the CEO of a company, or an entrepreneur stating a company, you cannot optimize for any one attribute. The minute you do that, you compromise your ability to perform at a high level in another area. . . .

The job of running a complex organization or starting a business is all about four or five different things that have nothing in common. So being a good manager, and optimizing the performance of any aspect of your company, is often at odds. . . . Being a good manager means saying to your employees, "You do it. You take responsibility," even though, by definition, they're not as good at it as you are.

My editor at the *New Yorker* magazine, David Remnick, is a better writer than 95 percent of the people who work for him. He's constantly in this position of having to accept articles that are not as good as the ones he would write himself. If he were to be completely honest and say, "I can't accept this," he wouldn't have a magazine.

That's the triathlon problem. At a certain point I have to say, "I can't optimize for being an amazing runner because I have to worry about swimming or cycling."

That's the same problem you face every day. Pay too much attention to any one aspect of your job and other aspects suffer. Work too hard on one area of your business and other areas suffer. Work too hard on any one aspect of your life and other aspects suffer.

That's why it's so hard to be world-class at anything . . . much less at several things.

And that's why you don't need to be world-class. Get to the 90 or 95 percent level in any pursuit and you will be extremely successful and will feel incredibly good about yourself. Perfection definitely isn't required.

GENERALISTS TRUMP SPECIALISTS IN TODAY'S PROFESSIONAL LANDSCAPE

In fact, the pursuit of perfection is the enemy. That's even true on a professional level. The current professional landscape values generalists over specialists. Change occurs quickly. Skills that are valued today are obsolete tomorrow. Managers can't just be good at managing a certain function; they need to be good leaders. Employees can't just be good at performing a certain function; they need to embrace an entrepreneurial mind-set and constantly reinvent themselves. When specific knowledge is more and more a commodity—and it is, because information is more widely available than ever—the people who can synthesize and blend and apply a broad base of skills to a variety of functions and problems are the people who are most valued. (More on that in a moment.)

It's Okay to Be a Tortoise

But don't stress about learning to code and mastering Mandarin at the same time.

Take a step back and think about your life in stages. If you're thirty years old, barring any unforeseen encounters with Gladwell's hair from which you do not escape, you should live to be approximately eighty—and that means you have eight to ten five- to seven-year periods ahead of you.

That means you have eight to ten different phases of your life that you can use to accomplish eight to ten huge goals.

For the sake of argument let's say that, even though you can train for a marathon in a year or two, it does take you five to seven years to accomplish your goal. That seems like a long time—but it's not.

Even if five to seven years are required to accomplish each goal, you have enough time to become a *serial achiever*: a person who accomplishes *this*, then *that*, then *that*, then *that* . . . all while working hard to succeed and advance in your career.

That means you can become an "and": a person who is this, *and* this, *and* this, *and* this.

A great example is Venus Williams. She's a highly accomplished tennis player, ranked the world's number one tennis player on three separate occasions, winner of seven Grand Slam singles titles, winner of fourteen Grand Slam doubles championships, four-time Olympic gold medalist . . . I could go on and on. Her legacy as one of the all-time tennis greats is assured.

What you may not know is that Venus has quietly crafted a successful career as an entrepreneur, launching her active-wear brand EleVen, a company that makes tennis clothing and performance women's clothing for yoga, fitness, running, and dance.

EleVen is anything but a celebrity vanity project: Venus is heavily involved in design, planning, operations, marketing . . . She even personally packages some orders (and when she does, she includes a card that reads PACKED BY VENUS).

That makes Venus Williams, like many highly successful people, a serial achiever. It's trendy to say the path to success lies in focusing on just one thing. Venus has never felt she should focus only on tennis: She feels she can be a tennis player *and* a student (she's pursuing a master's degree in interior architecture) *and* a designer *and* an entrepreneur.

Because most professional athletes focus solely on their sport, I asked her why she approaches her life differently.

"To me, that's normal," she said. "From an early age, I had to figure out how to be amazing at what I did and do well in school at the same time. In my home, we weren't allowed just to be athletes. We had to be students. And our dad taught us to be entrepreneurs.

"We would drive to a tennis tournament somewhere, and he would put in a cassette about buying foreclosure properties. We were eight and nine years old and we had to listen to how to make money on foreclosures. Obviously we didn't understand much of it. That didn't really matter, because our dad was trying to establish that mind-set of multitasking, of being an entrepreneur, of charting your own path. . . . So for me, trying to excel at multiple things is normal.

"I also realized early on that even the longest athletic

careers are actually really short. When you're an athlete, you're 'done' early in life, so I decided to see that not as a limitation but as an opportunity. So I've always been focused on having goals beyond tennis."

I know what you're thinking: "That's fine for Venus . . . but I just don't have the time to do all those things."

Um, bullshit. Yes you do.

WHY YOU MUST BE A *PROFESSIONAL* SERIAL ACHIEVER

Imagine someone asks, "What do you do?"

How do you answer?

Maybe you say, "I own a restaurant." Or "I'm a supervisor at a manufacturing facility." Or "I'm a teacher."

Whatever you say, your answer probably doesn't include the word "and." But it should—even though there's often a stigma associated with being an "and."

Take me. (Not because this is all about me but because I'm the only person I know a lot about.) I'm a ghostwriter and author. I'm a speaker. I'm a productivity-improvement consultant. Until recently I was a wedding photographer. And I take on physical challenges from time to time.

If I may say so—and what the heck, I will—I'm pretty good at all of those things (except maybe the physical challenges).

But here's what happens. Say I do a speaking gig. Invariably aspiring speakers will corner me afterward to talk about the business of speaking. Keen to fill in open cells on their revenue-projection spreadsheets, they ask how many speaking engagements I do.

"I try not to do more than twenty or so a year," I answer.

"Only twenty? Wow—you must get paid a lot for each event."

"It depends on how you define 'a lot,'" I say. "But I don't want to do more than twenty a year."

"Why not? If you did more events, couldn't you make more money?" they ask.

"Probably so," I say, "but I'm also a ghostwriter."

"What?"

"I'm a speaker *and* a ghostwriter," I say.

"Oh," they say, and their voices trail off as their perception of me changes. (And that's before I told them I also photograph about ten weddings a year.) After all, successful people do *one* thing. Unsuccessful people need to do a variety of things to make ends meet. If I'm a speaker *and* a writer *and* a photographer, then surely I must not be particularly successful at any of those pursuits.

So no matter what their initial impression of me as a speaker, no matter how big the event, no matter how sophisticated the audience, they no longer see me as a successful speaker simply because I don't speak on a full-time basis.

In short, I must not be good enough to specialize.

The same is true with ghostwriting. When I tell people I

also do speaking gigs, they generally assume I have to take on those engagements because I'm a struggling writer forced to find other ways to earn money.

To most people, professional "specialization" indicates accomplishment and success, when in fact the opposite is true. You, me, all of us—we're *too good* to specialize. Venus is too good to specialize. She is capable of more than tennis. She's too good to be just one thing.

None of us should be just one thing. We all possess, or can possess, a variety of skills—including skills we aren't using.

Don't say, "I can't afford to spend the extra time on an 'and.'" You can't afford *not* to spend the time. If your "and" is professional, then you create a buffer against downturns, shifts in market conditions, or the loss of a job. If your "and" is personal, you get to add a little more fun to your life.

And don't say, "I don't know where to start because I don't know where I want to end up." One of the biggest reasons people don't start doing, well, anything is that they think the first step must be a component in a comprehensive grand plan, one where every step is charted and every milestone identified . . . and because they don't have that plan, they don't start.

As Eagles guitarist (and eminent philosopher) Joe Walsh says in the documentary *History of the Eagles,* "As you live your life, it appears to be anarchy and chaos, and random events, non-related events, smashing into each other and causing this situation or that situation, and then this happens, and it's overwhelming, and it just looks like, what in the world is going on? And later, when you look back at it, it looks like a finely crafted novel. But at the time, it don't [sic]."*

And please don't think it's too late. Maybe you're smart enough to read this book and create a professional life plan in your twenties. I wasn't. I didn't have a clue. Neither did Joe. Read stories of successful people and it's easy to think they have some intangible something—ideas, talent, drive, skills, creativity, whatever—that you don't have.

Nope. Success is inevitable only in hindsight. Success is never assured. Plans are never perfect. Only in hindsight does it appear that way. What really happens is that people do things, try things, succeed at things, fail at things, learn from those failures, learn from those successes . . . and along the way they seize—and create—opportunities to advance themselves so they can live the life that makes them happy.

So go ahead. Be a professional serial achiever. Embrace your "and." Take the steps that let you include an "and" in the way you describe yourself professionally.

Think about what you do well, or would like to do well, and, most important, would really enjoy doing. Don't choose an "and" you feel you *should* choose. Pick a side hustle your inner

---

*Not that you asked, but my favorite Joe Walsh quote from the documentary regards fame: "The first thing that happens is that you get some kind of label, and you gotta live up to it, and you just get caught up in that, and I forget what the second thing is."

twenty-year-old will love. Being a serial achiever is a chance to explore, to delve, to expand, even to indulge—but with a purpose.

Maybe starting a small business on the side would be fun. Maybe teaching or consulting or working part time or volunteering or going back to school would be fun. It doesn't matter what "and" you choose, as long as it is something you really want to do.

Then you get to recharge and refresh, pick up new perspectives, and bring certain skills back to your primary role . . . or roles.

Keep in mind you don't have to start a totally new side hustle, or embrace a completely new interest, to be an "and." You can strategically choose to add new skills to your skill set.

If you work in an office filled with data-analytic superstars, you can work on being the best communicator—especially in meetings, where it's easiest for skilled communicators to stand out—in the building. Then you won't be "just" another number cruncher; you'll be the one person who can not only glean insights but also communicate those insights in a way that turns insight into action. (After all, data without insight is just data.)

Or maybe you work in operations and it's hard to stand out based on numbers and results alone. Fine, work to improve your sales knowledge so you can create projects that make the sales team's job easier: faster turnaround, smaller production lots, increased product options, etc. When the sales folks are on your side, you're impossible to ignore.

Plans are great, but plans without action are just dreams.

Pick something you want to do and try it. As Seth Godin says, once you had to wait: to be accepted, to be promoted, to be selected . . . to somehow be "discovered." Not anymore. Access is nearly unlimited; you can connect with almost anyone through social media. You can publish your own work, distribute your own music, create your own products, or attract your own funding.

You can do almost anything you want—and you don't need to wait for someone else to help you.

The only thing holding you back is you—and your willingness to try. Try something. Try *anything*. And trust that you're smart enough to decide whether it is right—or how you can make it right—for you.

Then you'll be an "and." Scratch that: Then you'll be a professional serial achiever. Then you'll have a number of "ands" included in the way you describe yourself.

I promise it will be worth it. After all, in most cases what comes after the first "and" will be one of the things you enjoy doing the most.

WHY YOU MUST ALSO BE A *PERSONAL* SERIAL ACHIEVER

Unless you're a trust fund baby or off hugging trees, professional serial achievement is vital. We all must make a living, and to some degree money is important. As Leonardo DiCaprio (as

Howard Hughes) says to Katharine Hepburn's family in the movie *The Aviator,* "You say money doesn't matter to you . . . but that's because you've always had it."

Of course, the need to make a living doesn't mean you must blindly pursue financial success. "Success" means different things to different people. (We'll talk more about your definition of success in a moment, because determining that is a crucial factor in choosing the goals you decide to pursue.)

Still, some people feel that their only major goals should be of a professional or financial nature.

Either way, do this for me: Take a moment and list a few of the things you've always wanted to accomplish—but haven't. Pick things that you regret never having done. Pick things that make you feel wistful to imagine. Write down three or four. I'll wait.

Now tell me: How many of the things you just wrote down are professional goals?

If you're like most people, none of them are. Not one involves career or money.

Instead, they're *personal* goals.

You feel less fulfilled because you haven't achieved them.

And someday you'll sit on your porch and deeply regret that you never did—and never tried.

The Best Goals Eliminate the Pain of Regret

As we talked about before, some of the worst words you can say are "If I had only . . ." Think about something you dreamed of doing five or ten years ago but didn't work to do—and think about how good you'd be at that thing today if you had. Think about all the time you wasted and can never get back.

Now project into the future and imagine you're eighty years old, sitting in a rocker on your front porch, reflecting on your life, regretting that you never tried to do the things you wanted to do . . . and now you never will.

A quote often attributed to Jim Rohn goes, There are two types of pain you will go through in life: the pain of discipline and the pain of regret. Discipline weighs ounces while regret weighs tons.

Sure, the work is hard. Sure, the work is painful—but it's significantly less painful than thinking back on what will never be.

That's why step two is to think about what you will most regret never having done. Keep in mind that nothing on that list will include work. No one lying on their deathbed thinks, "If only I had spent more time at the office." You may regret not having worked to find more fulfilling or enjoyable work, but when you're on your deathbed you will not regret failing to earn a more important title or snag a cooler office or make more money. Instead you'll think about what would have made you feel happier or more fulfilled.

When you're sitting in that rocking chair, you'll think about the things you wanted to *become*.

That's why personal goals are important not just to set but to achieve. Achieving personal goals, no matter how silly, how frivolous, or how impractical, is rewarding. And as you pursue those goals you meet new people, make new connections, build new friendships, and, best of all, feel better about yourself.

Those are all things we can use more of in life.

SERIAL ACHIEVEMENT MAKES YOU UNCONTAINABLE, UNPREDICTABLE, AND UNDEFINABLE

The beauty of serial achievement is that over time you become more than one thing. You can be a Web designer and a musician and an athlete . . . and then you can become something else as well, knowing that when you have achieved a certain level of skill or experience you can work to achieve something else.

Plus, the skill you gain will not be wasted if or when you move on to another pursuit. Except for unusual skills—like tech skills, which are constantly on the verge of becoming obsolete even for full-time programmers and developers—the skills you gain will stay in your tool kit. While over time you will naturally lose some degree of proficiency, you will always retain the core skill and will be able to quickly tune yourself up again if necessary.

Think of it this way: Strength is hard to build the first time, but regaining strength lost is much easier.

And even if you do lose a significant amount of skill, that's okay: The confidence and fulfillment you gain from all your hard work and dedication will in themselves make your effort worthwhile. You will always be able to look back and think, "I did *that*."

A moment of accomplishment may be fleeting, but satisfaction lasts forever.

HERE'S THE KEY QUESTION: ARE YOU HAPPY?

If I haven't convinced you that being a serial achiever is the best way to live a full, satisfying, and successful professional life and personal life . . . well, there's no hope for you.

(Okay, there is. There is always hope. Hope is one thing no one can take away from you.)

So let's take a second to talk about happiness, because goal achievement and happiness are inextricably intertwined.

As I said before, "success" in business and in life means different things to different people. It *should* mean different things. Each person is unique, so everyone's definition should be unique. Ultimately, whether or not you feel successful depends on how *you* define success—and on the trade-offs you are willing to not just accept but embrace as you pursue that definition of success.

We can have a lot, but we can't have everything.

That's why for an entrepreneur or an employee or a parent or a retiree—to anyone—there is only one way to determine success. The answer lies in one question: How happy am I?

How successful you feel is based solely on your answer to that question—and the trade-offs required.

For example, extremely successful—at least in terms of traditional business success—entrepreneurs work impossibly long hours while focusing almost exclusively on building their business. In many cases (some would argue most cases) their personal and family lives are to at least some degree casualties of that focus.

Is that a fair trade-off?

"Fair" or "unfair" is beside the point. Trade-offs are unavoidable.

If you're making tons of money but are still unhappy, you haven't embraced the fact that incredible business success often carries a heavy personal price. Other things are clearly more important to you than making money, and that's okay.

If, on the other hand, you leave every day at four o'clock and pursue a rich and varied personal life and you're still unhappy, you haven't embraced the fact—and it is a fact—that what you chose to do will not make you wealthy. Personal satisfaction is important, but it's not enough for you . . . and that's okay too.

We can try to compartmentalize all we want, but business success, family and friends, personal pursuits, no single aspect of our lives can ever be truly separated from the others. Each is a permanent part of a whole, so putting more focus on one area automatically reduces the focus on another.

Want to make more money? Want more time with family? Want to help others? You can, but something else will have to give.

The more money you want to make, the less happy you may need to be. The happier you want to be, the less money you may be able to make. In a perfect world, you could have full measures of both . . . but this is not a perfect world.

That disconnect is what causes so many people to spend their lives thinking, "Is this all there is?" That disconnect leads men in their fifties to wear gold chains and undo one too many shirt buttons and drive their new Corvette with the top down even though it's thirty degrees outside.

The problem isn't external. The problem isn't jewelry or clothing or cars.

You can't have it all . . . but you can have a lot.

But first you must know what you really want.

Be honest with yourself. What do you want to achieve for yourself and your family? What do you most value spiritually, emotionally, or materially? What do you most want to do? In what setting, or what pursuit, are you happiest?

But don't automatically say that your family and friends are the most important thing in your life. If they are, that's great, but if they're not, and yet you're spending the bulk of your time and focus on those relationships, then you're only cheating yourself out of the chance to be happier by focusing on what is more important to you.

(I used "family and friends" as an example for a reason. We're conditioned to say that—or we think it's socially correct to say that—but there truly is no right or wrong answer. If you're more interested in professional success than in maintaining close friendships, that's okay. You're not a bad person. You're just *you*. There is only *your* answer.)

Whatever your answer may be, that is what makes you happy—and if you aren't doing it, you won't be happy.

Sound too simple?

Maybe . . . but think of all the people you know who complain about the results of the path they have clearly chosen.

For example, we all know at least one high school teacher who constantly complains about low pay. I don't blame them. Teachers should be paid more. They have an incredibly important job.

But they *aren't* paid more. And unless something dramatic happens, they won't be paid more. As Marlo from *The Wire* would say, "You want it to be one way . . . but it's the *other* way." Teachers may be woefully underpaid, but currently that's the way it is.

If you're not happy, rethink your definition of success. The one you have is not working for you. You can't have it all. You shouldn't *want* to have it all because that's the best way to wind up unhappy and unfulfilled.

But you can have a lot more than you currently do, whether what you want more of is professional or personal success.

So start pursuing the goals that will make you happy.

MASLOW REALLY DID HAVE HIS SHIT TOGETHER

A guy in my neighborhood wanted to climb Mount Kilimanjaro. He hiked double-digit miles a few days a week. He spent hours and hours on a StairMaster. He carried around backpacks full of water jugs to simulate a heavy pack. He devoted twenty to twenty-five hours a week to training.

Good for him, right?

Not really. During that same time, his house went into fore-closure.

I know another guy who decided he wanted to become a chess Grandmaster. (The process involves a lot of study, playing a massive number of games, and constantly increasing your ranking by defeating better and better opponents until you qual-ify.) He was definitely dedicated: He spent nearly all his free time trying to become one of the few, the proud, the Grand-masters.

Good for him, right?

Not really. He got close . . . but then the combination of

weighing more than three hundred pounds and smoking two packs of cigarettes a day and getting zero exercise caught up with him; he had a heart attack and needed a double bypass, and his health is forever compromised.

Lofty goals are great. I love lofty goals. Unusual goals are great. I love them too.

Goals everyone else thinks are crazy—pursuits no one else but you may see as worthwhile—are great. We are all different, and so are our goals.

But in one way we are all the same. We all have certain basic needs. Maslow's hierarchy of needs lays out a theory that psychological health is based on fulfilling innate human needs in order of priority; fulfill all the "levels" and boom: You're self-actualized. I'm not as smart as Maslow, so my hierarchy is simpler: We all need to be healthy. We all need to maintain solid family relationships. And we all need a level of income sufficient to our needs. (Not wants, needs.)

Those things are nonnegotiable.

And that's why this logical leap isn't a leap at all: If you currently aren't healthy, don't feel good about your primary relationships (or the people with whom you are in those relationships don't feel good about you), and aren't making enough money, then you have no business taking on any goal that does not make one of those areas of your life better. It's impossible to feel fulfilled and happy if you aren't taking care of your basic needs.

And it's impossible to actively pursue a goal that doesn't take care of a basic need that is lacking, because you will always feel guilty about spending time on it. If you aren't bringing in enough money to keep food on the table and a roof over your head, you'll feel guilty and selfish if you spend time training to climb Mount Kilimanjaro. If you're overweight and out of shape and struggling to perform normal daily tasks, you might not feel guilty or selfish about working toward becoming a Grandmaster, but you should.

Sometimes it's obvious we're being selfish. Other times selfishness is harder to spot.

Take me. I'm not a "go to the doctor" kind of guy. I don't get regular checkups; I get a physical only when one is required for another reason. I don't go to the doctor for injuries unless my wife makes me; I figure time heals all wounds. I didn't even want to go to the hospital when I had a heart attack. (After all, the first sign of a heart attack is denial.) Luckily, I'm married to someone a lot smarter than me.

So where having a colonoscopy was concerned . . . no way. It was the last thing I wanted to do, even though colon cancer is the second leading cause of cancer death. And even though screening for colon cancer is recommended for people once they hit age fifty—because 90 percent of new cases occur in people fifty and older—and I was (cough) fifty-four. And even though colorectal cancer almost always develops from precancerous polyps in the colon. And even though a colonoscopy allows a physician to detect and remove precancerous polyps before they turn into cancer.

But I didn't want one. *Ick*.

Then my wife finally said, "I know you're rationalizing that you don't need a colonoscopy, but you're being selfish: There's me, there are our kids, and you now have a grandson. Lots of people want you to be around for a long time. When you think about it that way, are you really saying that getting a colonoscopy is just too much of a bother?"

Well, yes, in so many words that was what I had been saying.

So I got a colonoscopy. It was a nonevent. (It was even kinda fun to fast for a day.)

That's another thing no one tells you about goals. You may want it to be one way—the way that lets you pursue anything you want without regard to money or health or relationships—but it's the other way.

And it always will be. Just ask anyone who ignored the basics in his life (it's almost always men) to pursue a goal . . . only to feel empty and hollow because the "trophy" on the mantel came at too high a cost.

Happiness requires evenly balancing your multiple non-negotiable goals, blending in a negotiable goal where appropriate . . . and never, ever forgetting to self-evaluate along the way to ensure the balance never gets out of whack. For brief periods of time it's okay if that balance is off, but do that for long, and everything falls apart: your motivation, your confidence, your small successes—and ultimately, your happiness.

Because success isn't truly success . . . unless you're happy.

So yeah. Maslow had his shit together.

And so will you.

With my sermon complete, and sitting comfortably in the choir, let's look at the real requirements of a great goal.

1. The best goals make Maslow (and therefore you) happy.

To make it simple, answer these two questions.

Are You Comfortable Financially?

I know: "Comfortable" means different things to different people. For now, let's define "comfortable" as able to afford to pay your bills on time, eat healthy (not extravagant, healthy) food, provide for your family's basic needs, and consistently put aside a little money for retirement. "Comfortable" means you're not constantly worried about money and you don't constantly think about money. If you're constantly worried about or thinking about money, your first goal must be to generate more income, because money clearly matters a lot to you. (And there's absolutely nothing wrong with that.)

If you *are* comfortable financially, then . . .

Are You Relatively Fit and Healthy?

Fitness and health is another subjective category. My friend Jeremiah Bishop, a professional mountain biker, doesn't feel fit unless he is winning races. Of course, that's unrealistic for most of us. For now, let's define "fit" in a few key ways.

One, are you comfortable with your body? If you refuse to wear a bathing suit or bikini on the beach, then you don't feel fit. If you can't perform the physical activities you want to perform—or used to perform—and that bothers you, then you don't feel fit. If you're overweight and out of shape and on the road to major health problems (and though you may be good at putting that out of your mind, if you're honest with yourself you know that's you), then you're not fit.

But don't think of becoming fit and healthy as avoiding a negative; think of becoming fit and healthy as a massive positive. Feeling comfortable in your own skin and being able to do the things you want to do is not only fun, it provides confidence and self-esteem that spill over into every other area of your life.

Feeling fit and healthy isn't a luxury. Feeling fit and healthy is a basic need. Make sure you're taking care of your basic needs first—otherwise, no matter how much you may "want" to achieve another goal you choose, you won't. You won't have the energy. If one of these basic needs isn't being met, you will never get to harness the power of the feedback loop of success, where each small success gives you the motivation you need to keep going. That virtuous cycle, where Success → Motivation → More Success → More Motivation → More Success, will never start turning because you'll be distracted by greater needs.

And even if you aren't distracted, you'll feel guilty and selfish for putting so much effort into one aspect of your life while a basic need goes unmet.

Make Maslow happy and you will definitely be happier.

2. Your goal must benefit you on multiple levels.

Every goal should support multiple aspects of your life.

Say you've decided you need to be more active, but your health is relatively poor and you have to start slowly. And say you've always enjoyed gardening. You could buy a treadmill and stare at the wall while you walk . . . or you could plant a small garden. You could work in your garden. You could go to a local arboretum and walk the paths to get ideas for what you would like to plant. You could spend time outside rather than inside.

You'll enjoy the exercise. You'll look forward to the exercise. You'll get more active while enjoying a hobby . . . and the virtuous cycle of success, both in being more active and in watching your garden thrive, will motivate you to do more.

I realize that's a simple example, so let's go to the other end of the spectrum.

Kirk Hammett, the Metallica guitarist, was having dinner

with his friend David Karon. They were reminiscing about working together in the past when David helped Kirk design his line of signature amplifiers for Randall Amplifiers. They decided they should do something new together and chose to start an effects pedal company. (Guitar pedals change the sound a guitar makes; think Keith Richards's Fuzz-Tone on "Satisfaction" or Kirk's wah on, well, almost any of his guitar solos.)

"Do something new together" is a great goal, but it's only one goal. "Start an effects pedal company" is a nice addition. But Kirk extended it a lot further. He doesn't want to just make pedals—he loves the process of dreaming up new sounds and seeing them come to life. He loves asking other guitarists for feedback. He loves asking other guitarists what sounds they would like to hear, and then finding ways to make those sounds come to life. He loves applying new sounds to the music Metallica makes. Starting a business was also a way to express his creativity, connect with other people, and dive even deeper into something he loves—music.

"I've totally become obsessed with pedals again," Kirk told me. "What I would love to do is to create a pedal that's like the wah pedal or the Whammy pedal—something that becomes a go-to for a certain sound. That's what I want to find, and I believe we can do that."

Want to land more media opportunities? Developing a better delivery and presence will help, but who gets media opportunities? Experts. Become an expert in your field and you'll have something original or insightful to say—and your delivery and presence will naturally improve. Content trumps delivery every time. When you're an expert, you'll find it a lot easier to get booked—in fact, the media will seek you out.

Want to build an amazing network? Don't think in terms of building a network. Build a list of key individual contacts. Think about every key area your business depends on: supplies, products, professional services, marketing, media, etc. Then work hard to build a strong relationship with one person in each of those areas. Build a connection with a lawyer. An accountant. The shipping clerk at your supplier's warehouse. Your FedEx driver. An influential analyst. Make it your goal to establish a key contact in each area of your business—with a person who won't just return your calls but will also enjoy hearing from you—and you'll naturally build an amazing network.

When your goal benefits you in only one way, it's much easier to quit, especially when the goal you set is something you want but do not *need* to do. When your goal benefits you in only one way, you get far fewer daily jolts of motivation from small successes.

When your goal works on multiple levels, you become what you do much more quickly because it informs so many aspects of your life.

Even the most specific and unusual goals can benefit you in a variety of ways; all you have to do is look for them.

3. Your goal must be unquestionably measurable.

I left this requirement until last for a simple reason. The best goals usually start with a vague desire—get in better shape, lose weight, make more money, start a business, change professions, be happier—but then get distilled into a clear, specific mission.

"Get in better shape" becomes "complete the Greensboro Spartan race" or "finish the Luray Sprint Triathlon" or "qualify for the Southern Regional CrossFit competition" or "run the D.C. Marathon."

"Lose weight" becomes "lose thirty pounds."

"Make more money" becomes, well, a specific financial target you wish to reach.

You get the point. The best goals are binary: They're so specific you can't help but know whether you have achieved them or not. They're also based on an activity, not a hard-to-quantify state of mind or state of being. "Better shape" means nothing; "run the D.C. Marathon" means not just running any marathon—easier or harder—but running the Marine Corps Marathon held in Washington, D.C.

Fuzzy goals are meaningless.

The best goals are goals you can see and taste and visualize in great detail, because they're based on a real accomplishment and not a vague statement of intent.

NOW LET'S CHOOSE YOUR GOAL

By now you may have already chosen your first goal. Simply thinking about the process of setting goals may have helped you settle on yours.

If not, take some time to decide what you want to accomplish first. Just remember: **If you are in financial straits or relatively poor physical condition, your goal must help you overcome that challenge.**

And if you're really struggling, just reach back and pick a goal you've had for a long time. Then you get a twofer: Not only will you achieve a huge goal, but you'll also eliminate a regret you've held not so dear for a long time.

Then, once you have your goal, you're ready to create a process that will ensure you achieve your goal.

I have a number you can choose from.

And all of them work.

CHAPTER 4.5

Wishing and Hoping Is the Most Unrealistic Approach of All

I know. I said we were ready to stop talking and start *doing*.

But there is one last thing about goals that we need to discuss. It's so important, so foundational, it deserves its own chapter.

In the dictionary the word "idea" is categorized as a noun. But "idea" should really be a verb, because an idea does not actually exist until you turn your inspiration into action. I should know. I've had plenty of ideas but acted on few of them.

For example, when I was graduating from college, the fitness boom was still in its infancy. (I know. I'm old. But hey, someday you will be too.) When companies like Nautilus introduced the first widely available weight-training machines, strength training started to gain appeal for the average person. Layer in aerobics classes and Easter-egg spandex combinations, and millions of people started to work out.

I was in New York when I saw an early Nautilus demo. I remember thinking, "Hmm, there's a real opportunity here. I should open a gym." I thought about it a lot, scouted locations, talked to manufacturers and lenders . . . but thinking and planning was all I ever did.

Thirty years later, I still feel a twinge of regret whenever I go to Planet Fitness.

The same is true with computers. I owned one of the first Kaypro II "portables." (It weighed about twenty-five pounds, but technically it was portable.)

I was far from a programmer, but I did know more about computers than many people, and when IBM-compatible computers started to hit the market, I thought seriously about opening a retail store. (Remember, this was pre-Dell.) One manufacturer was even willing to front most of the capital because the company was trying to build storefront distribution channels.

Though in retrospect the opportunity would have been relatively short-lived, for about ten years that business might have thrived . . . if I had done more than just think about it, that is.

The list goes on. Years ago, a friend decided the home health-care industry was poised to take off. He asked me to go into business with him. I thought about it a lot, even helped him flesh out his financials and refine his start-up plan . . . but I never pulled the trigger.

Today he has locations in fifteen cities. The only connection

I have with home health care is that I will someday be a customer.

Sure, I can console myself by thinking that hindsight is perfect. I can console myself by saying that I had no way of knowing how those opportunities would turn out. But those rationalizations are only partly true. Even at the time, I felt sure those were great ideas.

Instead of acting, though, I let "idea" stay a noun. I didn't make "idea" a verb. Fitness and computers and home health care weren't really ideas, because ideas without action aren't ideas.

They're regrets.

Every day, people like me—people like you—let hesitation and uncertainty stop them from acting on an idea. Fear of the unknown and fear of failure are what stopped me, and they may be what stops you too.

Think about a few of the ideas you've had, whether for a new business, a new career, or even just a part-time job. In retrospect, how many of your ideas could have turned out well, especially if you had given the opportunity your best effort? Would a decent percentage have turned out well?

My guess is yes. That's why you absolutely must trust your analysis, your judgment, and even your instincts—and act on that trust.

You certainly won't get it right all the time, but if you let "idea" stay a noun, you will always get it wrong.

You will never achieve your goals if your approach is to wait. Don't just have a bias for action. Be active—be active doing the things that are most likely to help you achieve your goals.

If your goal is to become extremely wealthy, get started on your entrepreneurial journey. That's not a sure path to wealth, but it is the most realistic. If your goal is to advance your career, determine what matters most to your organization and start finding ways to make a quantitative difference in that aspect of the business. That's not a sure path to promotion, but it is the most realistic. If your goal is to drop a few pounds, for gosh sakes stop eating more calories than you burn. That is the sure path to weight loss.

Set a goal.

Then look at what is *required* to achieve that goal. What you need to do may not be what you want to do, and that's okay. Let everyone else take an unrealistic approach and then wonder why they aren't achieving more.

Be "unrealistic" when you set a goal, and then be realistic about how you will achieve that goal.

Then your goal will become realistic, because you have a plan in place that will allow you to achieve that goal.

Dream as big as you like. Then make sure your plan matches your dream.

So *now* let's get started!

CHAPTER 5

To Gain Incredible Willpower ...
Need Less Willpower

The purpose of this book is to help you achieve huge goals. But accomplishing a huge goal takes time.

So let's start small. Success → Motivation → More Success → More Motivation creates an awesomely virtuous cycle, so why not gain some immediate successes that will motivate you to knock off even bigger goals?

And while we're at it, let's do so in a way that helps you develop an attribute most people feel they struggle with—willpower—and, in the process, make willpower irrelevant.

Are we trying to accomplish multiple things at once? Absolutely. The best processes not only let you achieve an immediate goal but also help you gain skills and confidence that allow you to achieve other goals.

So let's start simple and lay out a strategy you can begin using tomorrow.

HOW TO HAVE YOUR MOST PRODUCTIVE DAY *EVER*

What if you need to complete a major project? What if you need to tackle a task you've been putting off? What if you desperately need to crank out a ton of work in a short period of time, yet you never seem able to find that time? What if you need to declutter your house or turn your backyard jungle into a paradise or . . . Shoot, you pick the task, professional or personal.

What we need is a Monster Energy Extreme Productivity Day™. (Okay, it's not actually trademarked, nor is Monster Energy currently sponsoring me . . . but hey, I'm always open to opportunities.)

Keep in mind that the following doesn't make sense as an everyday routine. Try to channel your inner Marissa Mayer and you'll flame out in a matter of days. But on an occasional basis, an Extreme Productivity Day (okay, I've already given up hoping the folks from Monster Energy will call) is the perfect cure for the "I am never going to get this done" flu.

Let's say you have a major task that will take you eleven or twelve hours to complete. Here are the steps to get everything done in one day.

Step 1: Let everyone know you won't be available.

Interruptions are productivity killers, so letting people know you're doing something special and will be out of reach for a day is an absolute must.

At a minimum, tell coworkers and family, but don't forget to tell important clients or other people who normally expect you to respond to them. Send an e-mail a couple days before your EPD. Explain that you will be tied up on that day and you'll respond to their calls, e-mails, etc. first thing the following morning.

Some people will contact you before your EPD; others will mentally note that you can't be reached. Either way, it's all good.

And you get an additional benefit from telling certain people what you plan to do that day. The people whose opinion you value will know what you intend to accomplish . . . and they will know if you don't succeed. Peer pressure—when applied to accomplishing a short-term task and not a huge, Appalachian Trail–worthy goal—can be a great motivator. Use it.

PEER PRESSURE DOESN'T HAVE TO BE PRESSURE

Quick note about peer pressure: The influence others have on you doesn't have to manifest in the form of pressure. Katheryn Winnick is the star of the TV series *Vikings*. She plays fan favorite Queen Lagertha, and she's also the queen of making plans. "I strongly believe in life plans," she told me. "I've been working on a life plan since I was fourteen. I set goals and keep them on my desktop so whenever I open it they're right in front of me. Some of the things I've dreamed about have come true. I'm an actress. I've been able to help women; I'm working with different charities to help support young girls and women. . . . All of those things are a part of my life plan.

"Recently I even hosted a vision-board party. I don't know if those exist; I just asked some of my friends over and each of them used words and pictures to put together their dreams and goals."

When I told my wife about Katheryn's vision-board party (I couldn't help but share, because it's the coolest idea ever), she got a group of friends together and held her own. They loved it—but she made sure the outcome was not just dreams but concrete plans to accomplish goals.

Step 2: Decide how long you will work.

Don't create a plan based on "I'll work as long as I can" or "I'll work as long as I feel productive." Set a concrete target. Commit to working for twelve hours, or however long a time frame you choose.

Why? For one thing, an EPD isn't about how you feel. An EPD is about getting things done, not wimping out because you get bored or tired. Two, the longer the time frame you set, the quicker the early hours seem to go by.

When I worked in a factory, we typically worked eight-hour shifts. The hours before lunchtime dragged, and the last couple of hours of each day always felt like death. But when we worked twelve-hour shifts, the morning hours somehow seemed to fly by. Something about knowing you'll be working for a long time allows you to stop checking the clock; it's as if you naturally find your Zen (work)place.

When you know you're in for a long haul, your mind automatically adapts. Trust me. It works.

Step 3: Totally commit to how long you decided to work.

You know what happens: Once you decide a task should take four hours, it somehow ends up taking four hours, even when it should actually have taken only two hours. It's natural to fill extra time with "stuff." (Think of it as the "bigger house syndrome," where we somehow manage to fill a much larger house with furniture . . . and then think we need an even bigger house.)

The opposite happens when a deadline seems too aggressive: We find ways to strip out the nonessential and get things done much more quickly than we could have imagined.

Don't just set a deadline. Totally commit to hitting that deadline.

And feel free to play any mental games that help. Make a bet with someone else, or make a bet with yourself (where "losing" means you have to do something you really don't want to do). In short, make the stakes personal. Find a way to be invested in the outcome not just professionally but personally.

Step 4: Start your EPD at an unusual time.

Have you ever taken a long car trip and left at 3:00 or 4:00 a.m.? The first few hours always fly by, because you stepped outside your norm. The same trick works for an EPD. Start at 4:00 a.m. Or indulge your inner night owl, starting at 6:00 p.m. and working through the night. Either way, those first few hours will fly by.

An EPD is not a normal day. Set the stage for atypical by breaking free of your usual routine.

Step 5: Delay and space out your rewards.

Say you like to listen to music when you work. On an EPD, keep the music turned off for the first few hours. That way, when your motivation starts to flag, a little music will provide a great boost to your morale.

Whatever ways you typically tend to "treat" yourself, think of those treats as personal productivity bullets. If you use all your ammunition too early, you'll have nothing left when you really need it. Whatever typically carries you through your workday, hold off on it for a while.

Delayed gratification is always better gratification—and better motivation.

Step 6: Refuel before you think you need to refuel.

When you're exercising, waiting until you're thirsty to get a drink means you're already dehydrated.

The same is true when you work. Plan to eat or snack a little earlier than normal. If you sit while you work, stand up long before your butt gets numb. If you stand, sit long before your legs start to ache. When you allow yourself to feel discomfort, your motivation and resolve will weaken—so do everything possible to keep that from happening.

Speaking of food, plan meals wisely. Don't take an hour-long lunch break. Prepare food you can eat quickly without lots of organizing or a mess. The key is to refuel, recharge . . . and keep rolling.

Remember what Isaac Newton said: A productive body in motion tends to stay in productive motion. (Okay, maybe that's not a *direct* quote, but still.)

That's why you should . . .

Step 7: Take productive *breaks, not relaxation breaks.*

Momentum is everything on an EPD (and on every other day). Don't take a walk or watch a little TV or check out your friends' latest humblebrags on Facebook. You will definitely need to take breaks, but those breaks should reinforce your sense of activity and accomplishment. Pick a few productive tasks you like to perform—and gain a sense of accomplishment from—and use those for your breaks.

Spending even a few minutes in the land of inactivity weakens your resolve.

Step 8: Take your breaks at a counterintuitive moment.

When you take a break, don't stop when you complete a particular task. Stop in the middle.

That approach works in the middle of an EPD or at the end of a workday. The key is to take a break—or end the day—by leaving yourself a fun place to start back up.

Why? Stopping in the middle of doing something awesome—or stopping right before you'll *start* doing something awesome—ensures you'll avoid the temptation of procrastination. Stopping short ensures you'll ignore all the enticing distractions that inevitably pop up when your motivation has flagged. Stopping short allows you to instantly focus and concentrate when you resume whatever you were doing. You won't be able to help diving right in because you'll be too excited, and that initial enthusiasm will positively affect the rest of your day.

Here's an example.

Say you're Kevin Jarre and you're writing the screenplay for the movie *Tombstone*. It's late in the day and you just finished writing the scene where Wyatt Earp tells the bedridden Doc Holliday (played by a movie-stealing Val Kilmer) that he needs to leave for a showdown with Johnny Ringo.

Wyatt knows he's no match for Ringo. Doc does too. Doc desperately wants to help but is obviously too sick. As Wyatt leaves, it's clear they know they will never see each other again.

If you're Kevin, should you then jump right into writing the next scene? Shoot, no. You should save it for tomorrow—because that scene opens with Ringo noticing a shadowy figure walking out of the trees . . . and just as the sunlight hits the unknown figure's face, he says to Ringo, "I'm your huckleberry."

To our (and Ringo's) surprise, it's not Wyatt. It's Doc. (Sneak off to YouTube and watch that scene. I'll wait.)

If you're Kevin, how excited are you to write that scene? You can't wait, because it's a scene that will make the movie (and define the character of Doc). The words just pour from you.

And if you're Kevin, and you write Doc looking down at a dying Johnny Ringo and saying, "I'm afraid the strain was more than he could bear," you know you've nailed an awesome scene . . . and that success makes you want to keep writing.

Within minutes, success ensures that your day—and your motivation level—is made, all because you started your day in a very fun place.

If you stop after you've just finished something significant or major—if you stop when you feel you've crossed a finish line and are nearly spent—it can feel extremely difficult to move on to whatever is next, whether you need to do that minutes, hours, or even a day later.

Step 9: Don't stop until you're done—even if finishing takes longer than expected.

Stopping short is an easy habit to form. If you quit this time, what will stop you from quitting the next time? (Answer: pretty much nothing.) Quitting is a habit.

Staying the course is also a habit.

Make sure your first EPD is the first block in the foundation of a great new habit: achieving what you want to achieve.

Finishing what you start, achieving what you set out to achieve, also produces a fun side benefit. Accomplishing more than you may have thought possible unconsciously resets your internal limit on your output. We all have a little voice inside that says, "I've done enough" or "I'm exhausted. I just can't do more."

But that little voice lies. We can always do more. Stopping is a choice.

Don't just take it from me. Take it from Ray Care, whose twelve-year navy career included ten years as a SEAL. (SEALs are the kings of pushing beyond the possible. Basic Underwater Demolition/SEAL training includes the aptly named Hell Week, a grueling five-and-a-half-day stretch when each SEAL candidate sleeps a total of only about four hours, runs more than two hundred miles, and does physical training for more than twenty hours each day.)

"Here's the thing," Ray told me, "about being 'done.' When you truly have nothing left in the tank, you either black out, pass out, or die. That's it. Otherwise you have more in you. It's all about getting past your comfort zone. We always have more gas in the tank. We just don't *think* we do because no one wants to run on reserve. They don't want to go past what they think is their limit.

"Winning is a mind-set. Refusing to give up is a mind-set. When you learn that you can do more than you thought in one aspect of your life, you can apply that to every other area of your life. Get out and do things that are hard. Refuse to quit. Push past your comfort zone. Over time that ability will become a habit—and you'll accomplish a lot more than you ever believed you could. Success is a mental game. Learn to win the mental game and you can do anything."

An EPD helps you learn to win the mental game. An EPD automatically ratchets your internal limits to a higher level. And after a few EPD—maybe even just one—you'll perform better every "normal" day as well, because you will have unconsciously shut down that little voice in your head and raised your own performance bar.

And isn't *your* performance bar the only measurement that truly matters?

HOW TO HAVE YOUR MOST PRODUCTIVE *WEEK* EVER

Now let's go a little bigger. Let's look at making every week more productive. This time, instead of taking advice from me, we'll follow the routine of a successful CEO. Again, you can apply this to any situation, professional or personal; if you're a stay-at-home parent, your family is your job, arguably more important than any "work."

Jim Whitehurst is the president and CEO of Red Hat, one of the largest and most successful providers of open-source software. Before that he was the chief operating officer of Delta Airlines. Before that he was a director and vice president of Boston Consulting Group. So yeah, he knows a little about personal productivity . . . and, if it's one of your goals, how to climb the corporate ladder.

Here's what Jim does, and what you should try.

Step 1: Every Sunday, map out your week.

Every Sunday evening Jim sits down with his list of important objectives for the month and year. Those goals inform the upcoming week and help keep him on track. While long-range goals may not be urgent, they are important, and if you aren't careful, the important can easily be pushed aside by the urgent.

Then he looks at his calendar for the week. He knows what

times are blocked out by meetings, etc. Then he looks at what he wants to accomplish and slots those tasks into his to-do list.

The key is to create structure and discipline for your week. Otherwise you'll let things happen to you instead of making things happen. Otherwise you'll let "urgent" push aside what is truly important.

Step 2: Actively block out task time.

You already schedule meetings and appointments. Go a step further and block out time to complete specific tasks. Slot periods for "Write new proposal" or "Craft presentation" or "Review and approve marketing materials."

If you don't proactively block out that time, those tasks will slip. Or those tasks will get interrupted. Or you'll lose focus. Whatever the reason, important tasks will never be completed.

I love David Allen's *Getting Things Done* methodology, but success isn't based on getting things done. Success is based on getting *important* things done.

Step 3: Follow a realistic to-do list.

Once upon a time Jim created to-do lists, but he didn't assign time to each task. What happened? He always had more items on his to-do list than he could accomplish, and that turned his to-do list into a *wish* list. If you have six hours of meetings scheduled today and eight hours of tasks on your to-do list, those tasks won't get done.

Assigning realistic time frames forces you to prioritize. Assigning realistic time frames also helps you stay focused. When you know a task should take only thirty minutes, you'll be more aggressive in weeding out and ignoring distractions.

Step 4: Default to thirty-minute meetings.

Whoever invented the one-hour default in calendar software wasted millions of people-hours. Most subjects can be handled in thirty minutes. Many can be handled in fifteen minutes—especially if everyone who attends knows ahead of time that the meeting will last only fifteen minutes.

Don't be a slave to the default settings on your calendar tool. Schedule an hour only if you absolutely know you need an hour.

Step 5: Stop multitasking.

During a meeting—especially an hour-long meeting—it's tempting to take care of a few mindless tasks. (Who hasn't cleaned up their in-box during a meeting?) The problem is that splitting your focus makes those meetings less productive.

Even though you're only doing mindless stuff, still, you're distracted. And that makes you less productive.

Multitasking is a personal-productivity killer. Don't try to do two things sort of well. Do one thing really, really well.

Step 6: Obsess about leveraging "edge" time.

Probably like you, Jim's biggest downtimes during the workday come when he drives to work, when he drives home, and when he's in airports.

He focuses extremely hard on how to productively use that time. He almost always schedules calls for his drive to work. It's easy: He takes the kids to school and drops them off at a specific time; then he can do a call from eight to eight thirty. He typically doesn't schedule calls for the drive home so he can use that time to return calls he missed during the day, especially to people who are on the West Coast.

At the airport he uses Pocket, a browser plug-in that downloads articles. Loading ten articles ahead of time ensures that he has plenty to read—plenty he *wants* to read—while he's waiting in the security line.

Look at your day. Identify the downtimes. Then schedule productive things you can do during that time. Call it "edge time"—because using it well can create a major productivity edge.

Step 7: Track your time.

Once you start tracking your time, you'll be amazed by how much time you spend doing stuff that isn't productive. (You don't have to get hyperspecific. The info you log can be a summary of activities, not a minute-to-minute diary.)

Tracking time was an eye-opening experience for Jim—and one that has really helped him focus.

Step 8: Be thoughtful about lunch.

Your lunch may take an hour. Or thirty minutes. Or ten minutes. However long it takes, be thoughtful about what you do.

If you like to eat at your desk and keep chugging, great. But if you benefit from using the break to recharge, lunch is one time when multitasking is in fact productive: You can network, make connections, build bridges between people and departments. But not if you go out to lunch with the same people every day.

Pick two days a week to go out with people you don't know well. Or take a walk. Or do something personally productive.

Say you take an hour for lunch each day; that's five hours a week. Be thoughtful about how you spend all those hours. You don't have to work, but you should make whatever you do work for *you*.

Step 9: Protect your family time.

Jim admits he's something of a workaholic. (I know very few CEOs—in fact, I know *no* CEOs—who are not workaholics.) So he's become very thoughtful about his evenings. When he gets home from work, it's family time: They have dinner as a family and he and his wife help the kids with their homework. He completely shuts off work: no phone, no e-mail.

Generally speaking, Jim has two hours before the kids need to get ready for bed. During that time he's *there*. Then he can switch back on. He's comfortable leaving work at five or five thirty because at eight or nine o'clock, he knows he will be able to reengage with work.

Every family has peak times when its members can best interact. If you don't proactively free up that time, you will often slip back into work mode. Either be working or be home with your family. Don't just "be there." Be *with* your family.

Step 10: Start every day right.

Jim exercises first thing in the morning, partly to stay fit but also because exercise is energizing. Research shows that moderate aerobic exercise can improve your mood for up to twelve hours—so why not exercise first thing and take advantage of being in a good mood for the rest of the day? Research also shows that exercise boosts energy; why not take advantage of a natural energy surge when you probably need it the most?

Jim gets up early and runs. Then he cools off while he reads the newspaper, and he gets downstairs before his kids do so he can eat breakfast with them.

Try it. Not only will you get an energy boost from exercising when you wake up, but being efficient and productive in the morning will set the stage for the rest of your day. Getting something productive done right away is fun, and it's motivating. Success → Motivation → More Success → More Motivation . . . so why not get your virtuous cycle started right away?

QUICK SIDETRACK: HOW TO HAVE THE MOST PRODUCTIVE *MIND-SET* EVER

So far we've looked at things you can start doing to help you achieve more, and to generate the motivation to keep achieving even more.

But sometimes subtraction is the best addition. Sometimes what you stop doing can be just as effective as what you start doing differently.

Want to get more done than the average person? Stop thinking the way the average person does.

Step 1: Stop making excuses for doing less.

Norman Mailer said, "Being a real writer means being able to do the work on a bad day."

Say you're a manager. When you're having a bad day, are you a great leader? If not, you're not a real leader. Or say you're a nurse. When you're having a bad day, are you as focused, as attentive, and as caring? If not, you're a nurse in title, not in fact.

If you want to succeed, you can't make excuses. Forge ahead. Establishing great habits takes considerable time and effort. Success and achievement are habits, and it's incredibly easy to instantly create a bad habit by giving in, even just once.

Plus, the moment you make an excuse for doing less is the moment you stop the virtuous cycle of motivation in its tracks. Without achievement, there is no motivation.

There are just excuses.

Step 2: Stop letting disapproval, or even scorn, stand in your way.

Work too hard, strive too hard, appear to be too ambitious, try to stand out from the crowd . . . It's a lot easier, and much more comfortable, to reel it in so that you fit in.

Pleasing the (average-performing) crowd is something you simply can't worry about. (You may think about it, but then you have to keep pushing forward. And yes, I know, that's hard. I struggle with it too.)

To succeed, hear the criticism, take the shots, endure the laughter or derision or even hostility—and stick to measuring yourself and your efforts by your own standards.

Seemingly every successful person has faced tremendous criticism and rejection. Stephen King's first book was rejected by thirty different publishers. Soichiro Honda flunked his interview with Toyota and decided to make scooters. Lucille Ball was told by acting teachers to try another profession. If you're trying to do something different—if you're trying to *be* different—other people will think you're odd. That's okay. Do what *you* want to do.

That's the only way to achieve what *you* want to achieve.

Step 3: Stop letting fear hold you back.

An old client of mine is an outstanding and extremely successful comic. Audiences love him. He's crazy good. Yet he still has panic attacks before he walks onstage. He knows he'll melt down, sweat through his shirt, feel sick to his stomach, and all the rest. It's just the way he is.

So just before he goes on he takes a quick shower, puts on fresh clothes, drinks a bottle of water, jumps up and down, and does a little shadowboxing. He's still scared. He knows he'll always be scared. He accepts it as part of the process. Preshow fear is part of the deal. So he manages it—and keeps moving forward.

Anyone hoping to achieve great things gets nervous. Anyone trying to achieve great things gets scared.

To succeed, you don't have to be braver than other people; you just need to find the strength to keep moving forward. Fear is paralyzing, but action creates confidence and self-assurance.

Step 4: Stop waiting for inspiration.

Most people wait for an idea. Most people think creativity happens. They expect a divine muse to someday show them a new way, a new approach, or a new concept.

And they wait and wait and wait.

Occasionally, great ideas do just come to us. Mostly, though, creativity is the result of effort: toiling, striving, refining, testing, and experimenting. The work itself results in inspiration.

Don't wait for ideas. Don't wait for inspiration. Big ideas most often come from people who *do,* not people who dream.

Step 5: Stop turning down the help you need.

Pretend you've traveled to an unfamiliar country, you know only a few words of the language, and you're lost and a little scared. Would you ask for help? Of course.

No one knows everything. No one is great at everything. Yet most people soldier on and hope effort will overcome a lack of knowledge or skill. And it does, but only to a point.

Ask for help. Asking for help is a sign of strength—and is the key to achieving a lot more. Ask Dany Garcia, cofounder of Seven Bucks Productions with Dwayne "The Rock" Johnson. "One of Dwayne's keys to success is he can detach his ego completely and care solely about who has the best answers," Dany says. "He's extremely coachable. He's really coachable in wrestling; as an actor he's really coachable. . . . He's totally detached from the ego side of decision making. When you're talented and coachable and willing to find the best answer, no matter who has it or where it comes from, that's extremely powerful."

Take a step back and don't just decide where you want to go. What, and who, can help you get there?

Step 6: Stop stopping.

Successful people finish—unless there's a very, very good reason not to finish, which, of course, there almost never is.

HOW TO GO THE *TRUE* EXTRA MILE, SEINFELD STYLE

I know some of this might sound hard. I know some of this might sound too difficult, especially because very few people apply this level of focus and routine to their lives.

But take a step back and consider the following sentence; though obvious, like most truisms, it's also easy to forget.

Successful people are successful because they do things differently from other people.

See? Obvious. But also true. To achieve differently you must *act* differently.

Again, I know that sounds obvious, but look around you. How many people do you work with who get to work at nine (when almost everyone else comes in), leave at five (when almost everyone else leaves), take their lunch breaks like everyone else, half-ass their way through meetings and assignments and projects . . . basically do what everyone around them does?

You know plenty of people like that, right?

Yet they're the same people who complain because they don't get opportunities, don't make enough money, don't get promoted . . . basically because they get treated like every other employee. *But they act like every other employee.*

Why should they be treated differently? They *aren't* different. Yes, they're all individuals, but from a professional point of view, they're essentially generic.

Everyone says they go the extra mile. Almost no one actually goes there, though. And when someone does actually go there, they usually think, "Wait. No one else is here. Why am I doing this?" And they leave, never to return.

That's why the extra mile is such a lonely place.

That's also why the extra mile is a place filled with opportunities.

Hard work is a definite differentiator, but there are other

ways to be different. You don't have to come to work early. You don't have to stay late. You can make the extra phone call. You can send the extra e-mail. You can do the extra research. You can help customers before they even think to ask. You can go beyond just telling your employees what to do; you can show them what to do and work beside them.

Every time you do something, think of one extra thing you can do—especially if other people aren't doing that one thing.

Sure, it's hard. But that's what will make you different.

And over time that's what will make you incredibly successful.

For example, you could take the Jerry Seinfeld approach. (Yep, another Jerry example, and why not? You could do a lot worse than to emulate the most successful comedian of all time.)

In an interview with Scott Feinberg for the *Hollywood Reporter*'s *Awards Chatter* podcast, Seinfeld describes his keys to success—which, not coincidentally, are three keys to success in any field.*

To Seinfeld, success is based on "work and thought and preparation." Those are givens. (Those are also the building blocks of confidence.)

Then he adds three further elements:

---

*Available at: www.hollywoodreporter.com/race/awards-chatter-podcast-jerry
-seinfeld-923565.

Inspiration

You have an idea. You come up with something new, something original, or even just a different take or perspective on a product or service.

"That's kind of the easiest step if you're a creative person," Seinfeld says. "You get ideas. They just come to you. You can't create them. . . . You just wake up and your in-box has got something in there and you go, 'Oh, look at that.'"

Of course, as we've discussed, an idea without action isn't really an idea; it's just a dream. So next comes . . .

Execution

"Execution is pretty obvious," Seinfeld says. "You have the idea; now you execute the idea. Is this what you wanted to do? Is this a good version of what that idea was?"

According to Seinfeld, the execution stage is where most people stop. "They have a good idea, they execute the idea, and then they cross their fingers," he says. "And they really hope that it works, and they have lots of excuses ready for when it doesn't."

But then what?

Detail

"The third piece of success in a creative field is detail," he explains. "Obsessive detail."

If you think about it, success in every field requires some

level of creativity. If you aren't coming up with new ideas, new approaches, or new processes, then you're just doing what everyone else already does.

Detail, to Seinfeld, is as important as inspiration and execution; they're three equal-sized pieces of the success puzzle.

"This happens to every comedian every night," he says. "I have bits, I have jokes, they work, they never miss, it's a good joke, people like it, every time I say it in this way it always works . . . but if I just have a slight catch in my throat in the middle of one word, just that little thing in the first syllable, it's gone. It's gone. The audience is like, 'What happened? Did he get nervous? Or distracted? Something went wrong.'

"In comedy, jokes are extremely fragile things because they have to be exactly right to work."

That's true in every profession. Execution is important, but obsessive attention to detail—making sure you get it right, every time, for every colleague or boss or customer—is critical. Comedians can't afford an otherwise surefire joke failing, just as businesses can't afford otherwise reliable processes or products failing. Detail is everything.

And that's true even in a business where creativity is not just appreciated but required.

"If you were a guest star on my show and you came on for a week," Seinfeld says, "if you missed a word—one word—in the lines that we've written for you, you're going to get a look from me . . . because that's the way we executed the series."

You're only as good as you are today, right here, right now, in this moment, and that's why detail matters as much as, or more than, ideas and execution. A great idea is great only when you execute that idea *incredibly well*.

Granted, incredible execution requires focus and discipline— but what if you feel like you lack willpower? What if you have yet to tap into the power of Success → Motivation → More Success → More Motivation?

What if you're afraid that you don't have the willpower to be more productive for a day or a week, or to go the extra mile?

Never fear. Help is here.

HOW TO HAVE WILLPOWER . . . WITHOUT NEEDING WILLPOWER

Willpower isn't something you either have or don't have.

Willpower is sometimes a function of necessity. (There are lots of things you can do when your back is against the wall and you feel you have no choice.)

More often, willpower is a function of success. It's easy to stay the course when you feel good about what you're accomplishing.

Willpower is also a muscle that can be developed; the more you exercise it, the stronger it gets.

And that's great, but what if you need help doing the things you need to do right now? What if you can't wait for the virtuous cycle of motivation to kick in?

You're in luck. Here are some tips you can start using today to help you accomplish what you want to accomplish, without needing to possess incredible willpower—or, really, any willpower at all.

The process starts with designing your life so it supports your goals.

Step 1: Eliminate as many choices as possible.

We all have a finite store of mental energy for exercising self-control. Some of us have less, some have more . . . but we all eventually run out of willpower steam.

That's why the more choices we need to make during the day, the harder each one is on our brain—and the more we start to look for shortcuts. (If you like, call this the "Oh, screw it" syndrome.) Then we get impulsive. Then we get reckless. Then we make decisions we know we shouldn't make . . . but it's like we just can't seem to help ourselves.

In fact, we can't help ourselves: We've run out of the mental energy we need to make smart choices.

That's why the fewer choices you are forced to make, the smarter the choices you can make when you do need to make a decision.

Say you want to drink more water and less soda. Easy: Keep three water bottles on your desk at all times. Then you won't need to go to the refrigerator and make a choice.

Or say you struggle to keep from constantly checking your e-mail. Easy: Turn off all your alerts. Or shut down your e-mail and open it only once an hour. Or take your mail program off your desktop and keep it on a laptop across the room. Make it hard to check—then you're more likely not to.

Or say you want to make smarter financial choices. Easy: Keep your credit card in a drawer, and then you can't make an impulse buy. Or require two sign-offs for all purchases over a certain amount; then you will have to run those decisions by someone else (which probably means you'll think twice about making the purchase and won't even bother to ask).

Choices are the enemy of willpower. So are ease and convenience. Think of decisions that require willpower, and then take willpower totally out of the equation.

Step 2: Make decisions tonight so you won't need to make them tomorrow.

It's also easier to make a smart choice when the decision isn't right in front of you. Pick easy decisions that will drain your store of willpower tomorrow, and make them tonight.

For example, choose what you'll wear. Leo Widrich, the co-founder of Buffer, found a way to make this decision incredibly easy: He wears jeans and a white T-shirt every day.

Or decide what you'll have for breakfast. Scott Dorsey, the

aforementioned cofounder of ExactTarget, eats oatmeal with blueberries for breakfast every day.

Maybe you'll choose to decide what you'll have for lunch. Just make sure to prepare it the night before. Or maybe you'll decide what time you'll work out. Just make sure to pack your workout gear the night before.

The key is to take as many decisions off the board as you can the night before, because that will allow you to conserve tomorrow's mental energy for making the decisions that really matter. The goal is to make certain actions automatic rather than decisions because decisions require willpower. The power of routine not only will make you more efficient but will also make it a lot easier for you to make important decisions.

When you don't have to make decisions, decision fatigue is very easy to avoid.

Regardless of what decisions you decide to make, here's one thing you definitely should decide: what you'll do first when you get to work. That way you can . . .

Step 3: Do the hardest things you need to do first.

You have the greatest amount of mental energy early in the morning. Science says so: In a landmark study performed by the National Academy of Sciences, parole board judges were most likely to give a favorable ruling early in the morning. Just before lunch, the odds of a favorable ruling dropped to almost zero.*

Should the judges' decisions have been affected by factors other than legal ones? Of course not—but they were. Why? They got mentally tired. They experienced decision fatigue.

That's why the best time to make tough decisions is early in the day. That's why the best time to do the most important things you need to do is early in the day. Decide what those things are and plan to tackle them first thing.

I know what you're thinking. What about the rest of the day?

Step 4: Refuel often.

Although the judges in the study started the day strong, a graph of their decision making looks like a roller coaster: up and down, up and down. Why? They took periodic breaks to eat or snack. Just after lunch their likelihood of making favorable rulings spiked. The same held true after midmorning and midafternoon breaks.

It turns out glucose is one of the foundations of willpower. Although your brain does not stop working when glucose is low,

---

*Shai Danziger, Jonathan Levav, and Liora Avnaim-Pesso, "Extraneous Factors in Judicial Decisions," *Proceedings of the National Academy of Sciences of the United States of America* 108, no. 17 (April 26, 2011): www.pnas.org/content/108/17/6889.

it does start doing some things and stop doing others: It responds more strongly to immediate rewards and pays less attention to long-term outcomes.

How can you avoid that? Um, duh: Eat healthy meals. Eat healthy snacks. Not only will you feel better, but you'll also make better decisions—and you'll be able to exercise more willpower in making those decisions.

And while we're talking about long-term outcomes . . .

Step 5: Create reminders of your long-term goals.

You want to build a bigger company, but when you're mentally tired it's easy to rationalize doing less than your best. Or you want to lose weight, but when you're mentally tired it's easy to rationalize that it makes better sense to start your workout program tomorrow. Or you want to better engage with your employees, but when you're mentally tired it's easy to rationalize that you really need to work on that proposal instead.

Mental fatigue makes you take the easy way out—even though the easy way almost always takes you the wrong way.

The solution is easy: Create tangible reminders designed to pull you back from the impulse brink. For example, a friend keeps a copy of his bank loan taped to his computer monitor as a constant reminder of an obligation he must meet. Another keeps a photo of himself when he weighed fifty pounds more on his refrigerator as a constant reminder of the person he never wants to be again. Another fills his desk with family photos, both because he loves looking at them and to remind himself of the people he hopes to provide for.

Think of moments when you are most likely to give in to impulses that take you further away from your long-term goals. Then use tangible reminders of those long-term goals to interrupt the impulse and keep you on track.

Step 6: Remove temptation altogether.

Every time you have to decide *not* to do something you would like to do—even though what you would like to do runs counter to your goals—simply rework your environment so you eliminate your ability to be impulsive.

Then you don't have to exercise any willpower at all.

Take the candy jar off the counter and stash it in a cabinet. Turn off all your social media notifications and check your accounts only every couple of hours. Take a different route to work so you won't be tempted to pop into Starbucks.

Or take the opposite approach. Put your running clothes on the floor by your bed so you'll have to put them away if you decide to skip your morning run. Keep your to-do list on top of your work pile so you'll have to move it—and ignore it—if you are tempted to work on something "urgent" but not important.

Finding ways to avoid temptation is a great way to avoid needing to exercise willpower. So is the guilt you'll feel when you are required to take a physical action to avoid making the right choice. (If your child is watching TV, it's easy to avoid reading her a story . . . but if she's standing in front of you, holding a book . . . ouch.)

As you know by now, the key to accomplishing your goals is to build the right habits and follow the right routines. When you control your environment, you make building those habits easy— and you make following the right routines as close to automatic as possible.

WANT TO GO BEYOND PRACTICAL TRICKS? LEARN THE PHILOSOPHY OF WILLPOWER

By now you know I'm big on processes, but I'm also big on mindset. The thought really is the parent of the deed.

So what can you do when you need greater willpower and perseverance, and one of the practical tips just described won't get you over the determination hump?

Take a step back and rely on the power of perspective.

Consistently doing what you need to do to succeed, with total focus and resolve, is incredibly difficult. That's why the ability to work hard and respond positively to failure and adversity is so crucial. Resolve, willpower, and determination help successful people work hard and stick to their long-term goals.

Want to develop those qualities?

Embrace the following mind-set.

Let Your Past Inform Your Future— but Don't Let It Define Your Future

The past is valuable. Learn from your mistakes. Learn from the mistakes of others.

Then let it go.

Easier said than done? As I said before, everything depends on your perspective. When something bad happens to you, it's an opportunity to learn. When another person makes a mistake, it's an opportunity to be kind, forgiving, and understanding.

The past doesn't define you. Just make sure that next time, you know what to do differently.

See Your Life—and Future—as Within Your Control

There's a quote often credited to Saint Ignatius of Loyola (and you have to love a fighting saint): "Pray as if God will take care of all; act as if all is up to you."

The same premise applies to luck. Many people feel luck has a lot to do with success or failure. If they succeed, luck favored them, and if they fail, luck was against them.

Most successful people do feel that good luck played some role in the success they enjoy. But they don't wait for good luck or worry about bad luck. They act as if success or failure is totally within their control. If they succeed, *they* caused it. If they fail, *they* caused it.

By not wasting mental energy worrying about what might happen to you, you can put all your effort into making things happen. (And if you do get lucky . . . hey, even better.)

Learn to Ignore the Things You Have No Control Over

Mental strength is like muscle strength—no one has an unlimited supply of focus. So why waste your power on things you can't control?

For some people it's politics. For others it's family. For others it's global warming. Whatever it is, you care, and you want others to care.

Fine. Do what you can do: Vote. Lend a listening ear. Recycle and reduce your carbon footprint. Do what you can do. Be your own change—but don't try to make everyone else change.

(They won't.)

Don't Just Aim for Tenacity; Aim for Adaptability

When you think about special operations personnel, the first word that comes to mind is "service." (As in, "Thank you for your service," because we all owe military personnel our thanks.)

The next word that comes to mind is likely "tenacity." SEALs, Army Rangers, Green Berets: Their training is designed to identify people who can stay the course, no matter what.

Yet tenacity is not their most important quality. Take it from Tyler Grey, an Army Ranger who was deployed twice to Afghanistan and twice to Iraq before being badly injured by an explosion in 2005 in Baghdad.

"With special ops," Tyler told me, "it's not people who are the absolute best at any one thing but people who are really good at a number of things. That means you have to be adaptable, because no one is good at everything.

"People tend to think Darwin said, 'Only the strong survive.' That's not what he said. Darwin said the number one survivability trait is adaptability. Adaptability is what will get you through these selection processes. Adaptability is the ability to recognize the construct and working mechanisms of a system, figure out how it works, adapt to it, and then adapt it to your needs and goals."

The thing is, you won't always succeed, at least not at first. Not if you're trying to do something difficult, something challenging, something *worthwhile*. So how do you get past the pain, the struggle, and the occasional failure?

"Discomfort is growth," Tyler says. "To constantly improve, and to be more resilient and adaptable, whenever there is a fork in the road, choose discomfort over comfort and you will grow. We're used to choosing comfort. We're used to choosing the easy way. Yet all our success and growth comes from choosing the hardest and least comfortable way. Say you're an entrepreneur: You chose the discomfort of giving up a paycheck and starting a company. Every success comes from taking the harder path.

"One of the best quotes I've ever heard says that if you want to increase the level of success, you need to increase the level of failure. There's a difference between quitting and failing. I'm okay with failing a thousand times. As long as you just keep going and don't quit, you haven't really failed."

Embrace that mind-set and you will *never* fail. You just won't have succeeded—yet.

Don't Resent; Celebrate the Success of Others

Many people—I guarantee you know at least a few—see success as a zero-sum game: There's only so much to go around. When someone else shines, they think that diminishes the light from their stars.

Resentment sucks up a massive amount of mental energy—energy better applied elsewhere.

When a friend does something awesome, that doesn't prevent you from doing something awesome. In fact, where success is concerned, birds of a feather tend to flock together—so draw your successful friends even closer.

Don't resent awesomeness. Create and celebrate awesomeness wherever you find it, and in time you'll find even more of it in yourself.

Resist the Temptation to Complain, Criticize, or Whine

Your words have power—especially over you. Harping about your problems always makes you feel worse, not better.

If something goes wrong, don't waste time complaining. Put that mental energy into making the situation better. (Unless you want to whine about it forever, eventually you'll have to make it better.)

And do the same with your friends or colleagues. Don't just serve as a shoulder they can cry on. Friends don't let friends whine; friends help friends make their lives better too.

Count Your Blessings

Before you turn out the light every night, take a moment to quit worrying about what you don't have. Quit worrying about what others have that you don't.

Think about what you *do* have. You have plenty to be thankful for. Doesn't reminding yourself of all the things you have in your life—all the things you would miss desperately if they were taken away—feel amazing?

Feeling better about yourself is the best way of all to recharge your mental batteries.

And it's the best way to be happy, because happiness is easily found when you appreciate what you already have.

Of course, happiness is also found in achieving your goals, so let's look at another simple strategy you can use to achieve a goal that takes more than a day or a week to accomplish.

CHAPTER 5.5

One Question Provides Nearly
Every Answer

Before we do that, start asking yourself one question—over and over and over again.

Think about what you want to become. Maye you want to become fit, trim, and healthy. Maybe you want to become a CEO. Maybe you want to become a business owner. Or a millionaire.

Only you can decide what you want to become. But once you do, you can't blindly choose how you want to proceed—not if you want to succeed.

To be a certain thing—to become a certain thing—you must make the decisions that will get you there.

Fortunately, making the right decisions is easy.

Just ask yourself one question.

That's how Herb Kelleher, the CEO of Southwest Airlines, makes so many decisions every day. Kelleher applies a simple framework to every issue: "Will this help Southwest be the lowest-cost provider?" If so, the answer is yes. If not, the answer is no.

The most effective people apply the same framework to the decisions they make. "Will this help me reach my goal? If not, I won't do it."

If you feel like you're constantly struggling to make decisions, take a step back. Think about your goals; your goals will help you make decisions.

That's why the most successful people seem so decisive. Indecision is born of a lack of purpose: When you know what you truly want, most of your decisions can—and should—be almost automatic.

Say you don't just want to exercise. Say you want to *be* fit. Then imagine you're out to dinner and the waiter asks about dessert. Would a fit person have dessert? Probably not. On the other hand, if you're a fit person who has run fourteen miles that day and burned a ton of calories, and dessert tonight fits within your routine and your process, then the answer is yes. Either way, you know the answer—without thinking.

And that means you don't need to rely on willpower or motivation, because you made the choice before the choice was ever presented to you.

Pretty cool, right?

Here's another example. Say you're saving money to buy an investment property. That's your goal. But you drive a 2009 Nissan Titan (that's me) showing some signs of age, and you see this incredibly sleek Jaguar F-TYPE, a car you've always wanted. (That's me again.) Technically, you can afford it.

Should you buy it?

Would a person saving money to buy an investment property buy a new Jaguar? Nope. Easy.

The list of examples goes on. Would a person who wants to become a supervisor, a manager, or a CEO treat other people with anything less than dignity and respect? No, because that's not the way good leaders act. Would a person who wants to be a good parent ignore a child who is struggling in school because spending time on social media is more—however oddly— gratifying? No, because that's not the way good parents act.

What do you want to achieve? Whom do you want to become? Place yourself there. Say, "I am fit." Say, "I am a CEO." Say, "I am a millionaire." Say, "I am a great parent."

You'll get the answer you need—and you'll stay on course to becoming the person you want to be.

THE FEWER THE GOALS, THE GREATER THE RESOLVE

Of course, that approach works only if you don't need to ask yourself multiple questions.

The more goals you try to achieve at one time, the more questions you need to ask yourself. More questions make the decision waters murkier. Murkier decision waters lead to greater decision fatigue and, as you know, overcoming decision fatigue requires willpower. Willpower is a finite resource; the fewer decisions you make, the less willpower is required.

Create the right environment and willpower isn't even necessary.

That means the key is limiting the number of goals you try to achieve at one time. Remember, you can be a serial achiever: You can achieve this goal, *then* that goal, then *that* goal. Focusing on one or two goals doesn't mean you're giving up on other goals; focusing on one or two goals means you're much more likely to actually achieve those goals—and then, later, one or two of your other goals.

And if you're in doubt, do this instead. Ask yourself, "Will this keep me from following my process?"

If it will, don't do it.

Process is everything. Routine is everything.

Let nothing stand in its way.

CHAPTER 6

Why Work Smarter When You Can Work Your Number?

One day I was chatting with two cofounders of a relatively successful company. They were whining about their inability to grow their customer base.

"It sucks," one said. "We have to call ten potential clients for every client we actually land."

I said, "Hey, that's great. Now you know what to do. If you need five new clients a month, create a system that allows you to call fifty potential customers. As long as you keep selling at a rate of one out of ten, you'll always hit your goal."

"That's stupid," the other said.

I wasn't fazed. I'm used to hearing that my intellect has been weighed, measured, and found wanting.

"No, it's not," I responded. "If you must get five new customers every month, that's what you need to do." (Yes, I also hold the rank of Captain Obvious.) "In the meantime, you should work to refine and revise and improve your pitch so hopefully you can someday turn that one out of ten into one out of seven or one out of eight. But for now you know how to reach your goal. You just need to do it."

Like the two cofounders, we often know, or could easily calculate, our "number." We just don't embrace it because thinking probabilistically doesn't come naturally. (I've always wanted to use "probabilistically" in a sentence.)

But when you think probabilistically, you begin to see success as the game it really is. Success is the result of rolling the dice a certain number of times. The more shots you take, the more chances you have of hitting the target. Working your number helps you predict how much failure you can expect on the road to success.

Why does that matter? Failure is inevitable, sure . . . but failure also sucks. Unexpected failure sucks even worse. But when you know that you'll fail a certain number of times, that's okay—because you also know that you will succeed a certain number of times.

That's how great salespeople overachieve. That's how great investors succeed. That's how great writers, great inventors, great entrepreneurs, great *everythings* succeed. Their success is based on skill, but it's also based on numbers.

Plus, working your number almost always results in improving your number. When you put in the work, your rate of return on your number steadily increases. Putting in the repetitions, while trying to increase the quality of every repetition, is fundamental to steady and lasting improvement.

Even if your goal is something kind of silly.

YES, I DID 100,000 PUSH-UPS (AND WHAT THAT MEANS TO YOU)

Working your number is based on consistently doing, over and over and over again, the things that make the biggest difference in your life. In short, working your number is about *grinding*: working hard every day to achieve your long-term goals.

To prove that—and to prove something to myself—in 2016 I decided to do a total of 100,000 push-ups and 50,000 sit-ups, in addition to my normal workouts.

I don't particularly enjoy push-ups. And I definitely don't like sit-ups. (Sit-ups can just fuck right off.) That was partly the point. The more you enjoy what you do, the easier it is to persevere.

So how do you achieve a huge goal when that goal involves doing something you really don't like to do?

Good question.

Here's the answer. Exactly 100,001 push-ups later (because hey, you can always do one more) and 50,000 sit-ups later (because that doesn't mean you *have* to do one more), the answer is that it was surprisingly easy.

Granted, I didn't do them all in one day. I didn't have to do 100,000 push-ups all at once; I just had to do 274 a day to hit 100,000 for the year. I didn't have to do 50,000 sit-ups all at once; I just had to do 137 a day to hit 50,000 for the year. The daily numbers were still big numbers, but they weren't *that* big, especially compared with the total. The daily number made the distance between here and there seem short. Setting a daily number meant "all" I had to do was go day by day, one day at a time, and grind it out.

As long as I stuck with my routine every day, success was guaranteed.

That doesn't mean every day went like clockwork. Most did, but several times along the way I fell behind due to illness or personal issues. I didn't fall too far behind, because most days I did an extra 30 or 40 push-ups and 20 or 30 sit-ups to build up a buffer against the occasional days that I knew I would miss. And at one point I caught up in a big way: I did 5,000 push-ups in one day. (How did that go? I have two words for you: It sucked.) I didn't do 2,500 sit-ups in one day, though. (No way was I going to do that.) Instead I added 50 sit-ups to my normal daily total until I caught up. (The nice thing about doing 190 sit-ups per day for a few weeks is that when I went back down to 140 per day, it seemed like I got done with that day's sit-ups relatively quickly.)

I also worked to improve over time, because working your number also means seeking to improve your number. At first it took me about thirty minutes to do 300 push-ups and 160 sit-ups. (I always rounded up to round numbers.) Within a month or so, I knocked four or five minutes off the total time. By the end of the year, a day's session took less than fifteen minutes, and that was without pushing myself. I could do all the sit-ups without stopping to take a break. I could do the first set of 80 push-ups with no problem, then continue with sets of 50.

To mix things up, and work on improvement, sometimes I did 30 push-ups at a time with twenty-second rest breaks in between, sometimes sets of 50 with forty-second rest breaks. After all, variety really is the spice of an otherwise boring routine.

Plus, and this is absolutely critical, improving—at *anything*—is always fun.

REPS ARE REPETITIVE BUT MUST NEVER BE MINDLESS

Years ago, Chuck Yeager, the first person to break the sound barrier, sent me on the wrong path.

Okay, maybe it was my fault. I read Chuck's autobiography and somehow came away with the (mistaken) impression that a good pilot becomes a great pilot by taking great risks. It seemed superior skills could be acquired only by constantly pushing the envelope, intentionally crossing the line between control and potential disaster and then reeling it back in.

I assumed becoming not just a good but a great motorcycle racer required taking great risks. Hey, I figured, I'd just ride WFO (wide-[expletive]-open), and by hanging out over the edge and pulling back in enough times, I would either become a great rider or . . . Well, I tried not to think about the "or."

Eventually—after far longer than it should have taken—I was forced to think about the "or" and realize guts had nothing to do with going fast. Maybe it was riding for another hour with (as I later discovered) two broken wrists. Or maybe it was touching an unpadded knee to the pavement at 120 miles per hour and seeing stark visual proof that a kneecap is made of bone. Or maybe it was when I realized I now thought of crashing not as an "if" but as a "when."

But what I did realize is that successful people are successful because they approach learning in a consistent, systematic, results-focused way. Bravery isn't a requirement for success. Innate talent isn't a requirement for success. Talented, highly skilled people don't take big risks . . . yet they still learn to accomplish big things.

How? They prepare. They train. They constantly experiment and adapt and refine, refine, refine. Highly accomplished people gain superior skills not by bursting through the envelope but by approaching and then slowly and incrementally expanding the boundaries of that envelope.

The key to learning is to make small, smart changes, evaluate the results, discard what doesn't work, and further refine what does work. When you constantly modify and refine a skill you already perform well, you can perform it even better.

Here are two proven ways highly accomplished people learn.

How to Do a Lot of REPS (Although Not the Kind We've Talked About)

Daniel Coyle's *The Little Book of Talent* is a cool book filled with easy and proven methods to learn to do almost anything.

Here's an example. Say you want to learn to do something. Simply going through the practice motions provides little or no results; the key is to make sure you use a system that follows Dan's REPS methodology:

R: Reaching and Repeating

E: Engagement

P: Purposefulness

S: Strong, Speedy Feedback

Let's take a brief look at each.

Reaching and Repeating

Practice should require you to operate at the edge of your abilities. In short, you have to consistently reach and constantly repeat.

You can also use this approach to teach students or develop employees. Say you're leading a training session. Should you . . .

- call on one person, ask a question, and have him or her answer it, or

• pose the question first and then randomly choose someone
to answer (and maybe even turn the exercise into a game)?

The second is the best approach because everyone will have
to reach every time—even those who aren't called on. Call on
John from accounting before you ask the question, and I know I
won't have to answer. I can sit back, check my e-mail, and wait
until you eventually call on me. I don't have to reach more than
maybe once. Always put yourself—or the people you're training—
in a position where you or they must reach, over and over again.
Don't just do what you already know how to do. Try to do what
you can't do—yet. That's how you learn.

Engagement

Practice must command your attention and make you feel emotionally invested in striving for a goal. Say you're trying to perfect your slide transitions for a presentation. Should you . . .

• run through the whole presentation ten times, or
• try to hit each transition perfectly, without mistakes, for
three presentations in a row?

Running through your presentation ten times in a row will
feel like death by about run-through five. Trying to be perfect
three times in a row turns the exercise into a game you care about.
Make sure the outcome of every session is something you

care about. You'll try harder and be more engaged, and you'll improve more rapidly.

Purposefulness

Practice must directly connect to the skill you want to build. (Sounds obvious, but often what we practice has little to do with what we need to accomplish.)

Say you feel nervous and intimidated when you speak to a group. Should you . . .

- rehearse at home, alone, until you know your material inside out, or
- practice speaking to small groups of people in less formal settings, like meetings?

Although solo rehearsing is certainly beneficial, the only way to perform well under the pressure of standing in front of an audience is to *actually speak in front of people*. No amount of solo practice can prepare you for the nerves you'll feel when every eye in the room is on you.

Strong, Speedy Feedback

Practice must provide an immediate and consistent flow of accurate information about performance.

Say you're studying for a certification exam. You purchased a sample test guide. Should you . . .

- take a complete test and wait until the next day to see how you did, or
- complete a section and immediately grade your answers to see where you went wrong (and right)?

Take the test in chunks. Check your results right away. Immediate feedback is the best feedback. You'll better connect the dots because you're in the flow. Waiting even a day for feedback creates a mental distance and a lack of engagement that is hard to overcome—which means that much of the time you spent trying to learn was wasted.

Pretty cool, right?

What If You Find Yourself in a Rep Rut?

Here's an easy way out—and another way to learn to do almost anything a lot better.

Try one—or all—of these:

GO SIGNIFICANTLY SLOWER.

Force yourself to go slower and you'll identify techniques or strategies that hold you back. Plus, you can experiment with new techniques that aren't apparent at normal speed.

GO SIGNIFICANTLY FASTER.

Force yourself to go much faster than normal. You'll screw up, and in the process you'll adapt and find new improvements.

BREAK A COMPLICATED TASK INTO SMALLER PARTS.

Almost every task includes a series of discrete steps. Pick one step, deconstruct it, master it . . . then put the whole task back together. Then choose another component to deconstruct. Incrementally improve enough steps and the overall improvement can be huge.

USE A DIFFERENT METRIC.

Pick a different measurement than you normally use to analyze your performance. Measure speed instead of accuracy, for example. Or use video or audio for feedback. (Watching or listening to yourself isn't particularly fun—in fact, I hate it—but you'll quickly recognize a number of ways you can improve.)

WHAT IF THE IDEAL NUMBER OF REPS IS "AS MANY AS POSSIBLE"?

Jimmie Johnson is a seven-time NASCAR champion (tied with Richard Petty and Dale Earnhardt for the most wins ever). But that's where he finished (though, as of this moment, he's definitely not finished), not where he started.

"When you look at any successful businessperson or successful athlete," he told me, "every one of them has work ethic. Work ethic is essential, but for me it was also the power of networking.

"When I was starting out, networking was the most powerful tool I had. My parents couldn't afford to take me racing. I had to meet other people, help other people believe in me, talk to people, know people, shake hands. . . . The whole networking process is what got me my chance to drive. Then I had to worry about doing the job.

"I was under the impression that talent would lead to opportunity, but really, networking led to opportunity. Networking came first—then I had to show that I could do it. I've always told my wife that for the longest time it was *who* I knew and not *what* I knew. Once I had my shot, I had to know my stuff, but who I knew was what really opened the door to show what I could do. But I wasn't 'selling' myself. I wasn't good at selling.

"When I was nineteen or twenty I was on a path to get into the IndyCar space and suddenly found out that if I wanted a future in motor sports, I needed to move to North Carolina and consider NASCAR. So I bought a plane ticket to Charlotte and lived on someone's couch.

"The first thing I did was buy business cards with my name

and 'Professional Race Car Driver' at the bottom." He laughed. "I found out where some of the team guys would eat lunch and every day I would show up at eleven o'clock. When people came in, I would introduce myself, shake their hands, and give them a business card. I asked if I could come to their shops, look around, learn about cars.... It wasn't about selling, it was about learning: I'm a driver and I want to learn.

"I went to every auto show. I went to every sponsor event I could find. I passed out my card, and every business card I received I sent a letter to that person saying how nice it was to meet them, I put them on my fax list . . . I had this whole system set up to try to keep my name in front of people. And eventually it paid off."

Jimmie didn't have a specific daily number to work. He worked at it every day, and his number was "as many as I can every day." His number was "send a letter to every person I meet."

That's a modified version of the "work your number" approach, one that lends itself well to a goal where the number of daily reps is at least partly out of your control.

For example, Aristotle Onassis, who built a massive shipping conglomerate, always carried a notebook. "Write everything down," he said. "When you have an idea, write it down. When you meet someone new, write down everything you know about them. When you hear something interesting, write it down. Writing it down will make you act upon it. If you don't write it down you will forget it."*

Richard Branson does something similar, except instead of writing down what he learns, he writes down his reaction to everything he learns, caring more about what he can do with the knowledge he's gained.

Sometimes the right number to work will be "as many as I can."

THE SECOND-MOST-REWARDING NUMBER TO WORK: THE ONE YOU OWN

If you're hoping to build wealth, you know how I feel about becoming an entrepreneur: Starting a business is the only way to have a chance to amass significant wealth.

Do yourself a favor and use the "work your number" approach to get started on that goal. Every day, commit to doing one—or more, if you choose—of the following until the list is complete.

When you're done, you may not yet have a thriving business, but you will have laid the groundwork. And you can feel good about having done something that many people dream about but never do.

Like my neighbor. He talked for at least six months about

---

*Drew Hansen, "Why Richard Branson and I Always Carry a Notepad," *Forbes*, August 15, 2011, www.forbes.com/sites/drewhansen/2011/08/15/why-richard -branson-and-i-always-carry-a-notepad/#416ce5586bea.

starting a business. Whenever I saw him, that was all he talked about. Eventually I got tired of it.

"What the heck are you waiting for?" I finally asked.

It turns out he thought the process of starting a business was really complicated. "I don't want to go through all that stuff," he said, "unless I'm absolutely sure my idea is perfect." Like a lot of would-be entrepreneurs, he was stalling because he was intimidated by the apparent complexity of the administrative and legal tasks involved in starting a business.

And he didn't realize that "idea" should always be a verb.

I bet him lunch that we could take care of all that in less than three hours. (I won.) And that means you can definitely commit to knocking off one or more of the following every day. Just keep in mind that I'm talking only about setting yourself up to do business; I'm not talking about writing a business plan, sourcing financing, developing a marketing plan, actually selling a product or service, etc. The goal here is to get off square one and get on to the fun stuff.

Here's your list.

Step 1: Get over the company-name thing.

Plenty of people endlessly agonize over dreaming up the perfect company name. Don't. If you're waiting until you come up with the perfect name, you're also waiting to start making money.

Instead, at least for now, forget branding and unique selling propositions and all that business-identity stuff. And don't worry about finding the perfect URL or Web site design or promotional literature. You're putting those carts way before your business horse too.

Just pick a name so you can get the administrative ball rolling.

Remember, your business can operate under a different name from your company name. (A "doing business as" form, or DBA, takes about a minute to fill out and file.) And you can change your company name later, if you like.

Step 2: Get Your Employer Identification Number (EIN).

An EIN is the federal tax number used to identify your business. You don't need an EIN unless you will have employees or plan to form a partnership, LLC, or corporation.

But even if you don't need an EIN, get one anyway: It's free, it takes minutes, and you can keep your Social Security number private and reduce the chance of identity theft, because if you don't have an EIN, your SSN identifies your business for tax purposes.

Note: If you're using an online legal service to set up an LLC or corporation, don't use it to get your EIN. Instead, apply online at the IRS Web site. (Search "apply for EIN online" and choose the IRS Web site from the results.) You'll have your EIN in minutes.

And with that, it's time to head to your locality's administrative offices.

Step 3: Register your trade name.

If you won't be operating under your own name, your locality may require you to register a trade name. In most cases, you'll be approved on the spot (unless you try to register a name someone else has already registered).

Step 4: Get your business license.

Your county or city will require a business license. The form takes minutes to fill out. Use your EIN instead of your Social Security number to identify your business (for privacy reasons if nothing else).

You may be asked to estimate annual gross receipts. Do your best to estimate accurately, but don't agonize over it. You're just providing an estimate.

Step 5: Complete a business personal property tax form (if necessary).

Businesses are taxed on "personal" property, just like individuals are in many states. Where I live, no form is required for the year the business is established.

If you are required to file a business personal property tax form and you plan to work from home using computers or tools that you already own, you shouldn't need to list those items.

If you purchase tangible personal property during your first year in business, you will list those items when you file your business personal property tax form the following year. (If you're unsure, spend a couple minutes on the phone with an accountant.)

Let me guess: This part stresses you out. Don't let it. I don't use business funds to buy any business items (computers, mobile devices, vehicles, office furniture, etc.). I buy all those things using personal funds. While that does prohibit me from claiming a tax break for those expenses, it also makes my accounting life a lot simpler. I don't have to worry about using any business assets exclusively for business purposes, I don't have to worry about any accounting involved in selling or disposing of those items. I willingly trade a business deduction for simplicity.

Whether you choose to do that is up to you (and your accountant), but just know that when you're starting out, you can keep things really simple.

Step 6: Ask your locality about other permits.

Every locality has different requirements. Where I used to live, for example, a "home occupation permit" was required to verify that any business based in a home met zoning requirements.

Your locality may require other permits. Ask. They'll tell you.

Step 7: Get a certificate of resale (if necessary).

A certificate of resale, also known as a resale certificate or seller's permit, allows you to collect state sales tax on products sold. (In some states, there is no sales tax on services.)

If you will sell products, you will need a seller's permit. The Web site for your state's taxing authority has complete details, forms, etc. if you decide to apply online, but most localities have preprinted forms you can complete while you're at their administrative offices taking care of other tasks.

Step 8: Open a business bank account.

A moment ago I advocated for simplicity—but I won't in this case. One of the easiest ways to screw up your business accounting and possibly run afoul of the IRS is to commingle personal and business funds (and transactions). Using a business account for all business transactions eliminates that possibility.

Get a business account using your business name and EIN, and use only that account for all business-related deposits, withdrawals, and transactions. Pick a bank or credit union that is convenient. Take a few minutes to check out your local credit unions; often they will provide better deals than banks.

Step 9: Set up a simple accounting spreadsheet.

Down the road you can worry about business accounting software, like QuickBooks. For now, just create a spreadsheet you can use to enter and track the money you spend and the money you receive.

Bookkeeping is simple, at least at first. All you need are revenue and expense columns; you can add line items as you go. Instead of spending hours playing with accounting software, dreaming up potential expense and income categories, and creating fancy reports with no data, spend that time generating revenue. As long as you record everything you earn and spend in your spreadsheet, creating a more formal system later will be fairly easy. It will also be more fun, because then you'll have *real* data to enter.

And what's even more fun is that now you'll be an entrepreneur, with all the documents to prove it.

And now you'll be motivated to actually *build* the business you just set up.

THE MOST REWARDING NUMBER TO WORK

Maybe you're still struggling to think of your "and." Maybe you're still struggling to determine what goal you want to pursue. If that's you, here's a perfect use for "work your number": Focus on other people.

That's the Jack Welch approach.

WHY WORK SMARTER WHEN YOU CAN WORK YOUR NUMBER?

There are many things you can say about Jack Welch, and this is one of them: Jack definitely knows how to develop great leaders. That was true when he was the CEO of General Electric, and it remains true today. For example, the Jack Welch Management Institute online MBA program has been named the most influential education brand on LinkedIn and was named a 2016 "business school to watch" by *Poets & Quants*.

As Jack told me, "Success is based on people first and strategy second. Build a great team and you will accomplish things beyond your wildest dreams. You grow from the reflected glory of your people.

"When your team delivers, you enjoy the fruit."

That's why, if you're struggling to think of a way to better succeed, to better stand out, to use "work your number" to achieve more, you should focus on other people. Focus on doing one thing every day to develop one of your people. Focus on doing one thing every day that helps one or more of the people around you to be better. Focus on doing one thing that helps you better use what Jack calls your "generosity gene."

"Early in my career, I wish I had then had a better definition of what I now call the generosity gene," Jack said. "For a long time, I never quite identified that ingredient. If a leader didn't desperately want to give raises, to promote people, if he didn't get as much satisfaction from other people's success as he did from his own . . . I didn't see that as well as I should have.

"I have never seen a great leader that didn't have the

195

generosity gene. Take care of your people, let them know where they stand, cheer them, never take credit for what they do, and they'll go to the moon for you."

When you think about it that way, deciding to use your generosity gene every day is an ideal way to work your number.

Want some tips?

Work your number by giving.

Give Greater Autonomy and Independence

Great organizations are built on the optimizing of processes and procedures. Still, every task doesn't deserve a best practice or a micromanaged approach. (I'm looking at you, manufacturing.) Engagement and satisfaction are largely based on autonomy and independence. I care when it's "mine." I care when I'm in charge and feel empowered to do what's right.

Plus, freedom breeds innovation: Even heavily process-oriented positions have room for different approaches. (Still looking at you, manufacturing.)

Whenever possible, give the people around you the autonomy and independence to work the way they work best. When you do, they almost always find ways to do their jobs better than you imagined possible.

That applies to your friends; if you ask someone for a favor, let them decide how they will deliver what you need. And it definitely applies to your kids; tell them what you would like them to do, but give them the freedom to figure out how to do it. Every parent's goal is to raise children who become independent adults—so start now.

Give Clearer Expectations

While every task should include some degree of independence, every task also needs basic expectations for how specific situations should be handled.

Criticize an employee for offering a discount to an irate customer today, even though yesterday that was standard practice, and you make that employee's job impossible. Few things are more stressful than not knowing what is expected from one day to the next.

When you change a standard or guideline, communicate the change beforehand—and when that is not possible, take the time to explain why you made the decision you made and what you expect in the future.

And yes, this definitely applies to your kids. Children seek independence, but they also crave structure and predictability. Provide both.

Give More Meaningful Objectives

Almost everyone is competitive; often the best employees are extremely competitive—especially with themselves. Meaningful targets can create a sense of purpose and add a little meaning to even the most repetitive tasks. Plus, goals are fun. Without a meaningful goal to shoot for, work is just work.

No one likes work.

Give a Better Sense of Purpose

Everyone likes to feel a part of something bigger. Everyone loves to feel that sense of teamwork and esprit de corps that turn a group of individuals into a real team.

The best missions involve making a real impact on the lives of the people you serve. When the people around you know how their effort contributes to the business, or to customers, or to the community, work takes on greater meaning. That's especially true when people are given the freedom to create a mission or two of their own.

Feeling a true purpose starts with knowing what to care about and, more important, why you should care.

Give More Opportunities to Provide Significant Input

Engaged employees have ideas; take away opportunities for them to make suggestions, or instantly disregard their ideas without consideration, and they immediately disengage.

Make it incredibly easy for people to offer suggestions. Ask leading questions. Probe gently. Help people feel comfortable proposing new ways to get things done. When an idea isn't feasible, always take the time to explain why.

Employees who make suggestions care about the company, so do everything you can to ensure they know their input is valued—and appreciated.

That premise is even more applicable to families; after all, employees expect to be told what to do, at least part of the time. Does your significant other? Do your kids?

Give a Better Sense of Connection

Employees work for a paycheck (otherwise they would do volunteer work), but they want more than a paycheck: They want to work with and for people they respect and admire—and who respect and admire them.

A kind word, a quick discussion about family, an informal conversation to ask if an employee needs any help—those moments are much more important than group meetings or formal evaluations.

A true sense of connection is personal. Show that you see and appreciate the person, not just the worker.

Give Greater Consistency

Most people don't mind a boss who is strict, demanding, and quick to offer (not-always-positive) feedback . . . as long as he or she also treats every employee fairly.

(The best bosses treat each employee differently while treating every employee fairly. There's a big difference between sameness and fairness.)

Consistency and fairness are based on communication. The more employees understand why a decision was made, the less likely they are to assume unfair treatment or favoritism.

Give Private Criticism

No employee is perfect. Every employee needs constructive feedback. Every employee deserves constructive feedback. Good bosses give that feedback.

Great bosses always do it in private. So do great partners and great parents.

Give Public Praise

Every employee—even a relatively poor performer—does *something* well. That's why every employee deserves praise and appreciation. It's easy to recognize and praise the best employees, because they're consistently doing awesome things. (Maybe consistent recognition is a reason they're the best employees? Something to think about.)

You may have to work hard to find reasons to recognize someone you work with who simply meets standards, but that's okay; a few words of recognition—especially public recognition—might be all the nudge an average performer needs to start becoming a great performer.

Give Everyone a Chance for a Meaningful Future

Every job should have the potential to lead to greater things. Whenever you can, whether you're a boss or not, help other employees gain skills or experience that will help them land the job they someday hope to land, even if that job is with another company.

While that might sound odd, training people to move on to bigger things outside your business is often how it works in the high-end restaurant industry. Take Eric Ripert, chef and co-owner of the acclaimed New York City restaurant Le Bernardin, author, frequent guest judge on *Top Chef,* and the host of the long-running series *Avec Eric.* (If you know anything at all about celebrity chefs, you know Eric.) Training people who not only will leave but may also become your competition is, how shall we say it, de rigueur in Eric's restaurant. (That's my nod to his French heritage.)

"Ultimately those young chefs one day will become better than us," Eric told me. The new generation that we see coming is already showing signs of extreme talent. It's a logical progression from generation to generation: bring the brick, they step on it, they go higher. My generation learned from the talent and the generosity of our mentors, and we did what we do today, and now there is a new generation. There will be many generations to follow that will do the same thing, and that makes us happy.

"It's nothing to be worried about," says Eric. "It's a natural part of life."

How can you know what another person hopes to someday do? Easy: Ask.

And if you are a boss, employees will care about your company only after you have shown you care about them. One of the best ways to do that is to not just say but show that while you have hopes for your company's future, you also have hopes for your employees' futures.

WHILE WE'RE AT IT . . . WORKING YOUR NUMBER CAN ALSO BE FUN

Success strategies don't have to be used separately. You can—and should—blend two or more together when doing so will result in greater success, greater motivation, and even greater success.

For example, let's use a time-specific form of "work your number" in conjunction with an Extreme Productivity Day. Let's choose a goal that might seem odd at first but proves that working your number can be applied to almost anything.

And let's learn, by my example, a few things *not* to do.

I started with a simple premise, one we discussed a few minutes ago when we talked about Jack Welch, the generosity gene, and ways you can be more giving. The idea was that no one gets enough praise. No one gets enough recognition. Few of us praise and recognize people as often as we should. I know I don't.

So in the spirit of challenging myself, I decided I would compliment every person I ran into for an entire day—even if I ran into them only in passing, even if I didn't know them, even if it didn't seem socially appropriate... and even if I had a tough time thinking of something (thinking of *anything*) I could compliment them for.

While that might sound easier than doing five thousand push-ups, for me it wasn't. I'm shy. I don't go out of my way to speak to people I don't know. (You might even argue that I go out of my way *not* to speak to people I don't know. And you might win that argument.)

Here's how *that* little experiment went.

My Rules

Challenges work best when you impose structure, helping you stay on track and reducing the temptation to lose resolve and rationalize that you should change your goal midstream.

For this challenge, the structure was simple:

- If I made eye contact with someone, I had to compliment them in some way.

- To make sure I never chickened out, I had to actively try to make eye contact. I couldn't intentionally look away.

- But I didn't have to compliment people who were already having a conversation or on the phone or wearing headphones. (I didn't want to be rude.)

- And I couldn't hide away all day. I had to go out into the world at least four times.

So with that in mind . . .

My Morning

The first few compliments were really easy.

I was rolling a trash can out to the street and saw my neighbor. She has a great collection of plants and flowers, so I said, "I'm always impressed by how beautiful your plants are. You have a real gift." Her face lit up. I don't think I made her day, but I do think I helped get her day off to a good start.

Then I went for a quick walk on the beach. Because this was fall, many of the people I met were walking their dogs or throwing balls into the surf for the dogs to retrieve.

"You have a beautiful dog," I said to the first person I walked by. He smiled, but I realized I had complimented his dog, not him. Although many dog owners don't see a difference . . . Still, rules are rules.

So I followed up with "She seems so happy. You must take

really good care of her." He beamed and I realized I was right: Complimenting a person's dog (or child or car or whatever) is nice, but complimenting the person makes a bigger impact.

So that's what I did. I told one man he had done an amazing job training his dog. I complimented a lady on how well she groomed her dog.

I was rolling. I felt pretty darn smug. This "compliment every person you meet" thing was easier than I thought.

Then, off in the distance, I saw a fit, pretty, twentysomething woman headed my way. No dog. No third-person-ish thing to compliment. Uh-oh.

I didn't want to be *that* guy, that older guy who goes around randomly complimenting young women and comes off creepy and, well, icky.

I started to walk more slowly. I thought furiously. But I had nothing. *Crap.*

Then, from about twenty feet away, she made eye contact and smiled. Not a half smile, not an automatic "good morning" smile, but a big, genuine smile.

I smiled back and said, "Thanks."

"For what?" she said.

"Lots of times when I'm walking people don't even make eye contact. I always think that's kind of rude. You saying hi to me was really nice."

She smiled even bigger and said, "How could I not be happy when I'm out here? Have a great day."

I know: What I came up with was lame. But I like to think she walked away feeling good about herself, if only for a moment or two, which was the whole point of the exercise.

And I felt pretty good about myself too ... at least until later, when I came upon a woman and her child and led with "Your daughter is really cute," only to be told, "Thank you, but he's a boy."

Oh well.

My Afternoon

Except for a few miscues, things were going well. I had learned to quickly size people up and pick out something obvious I could compliment: how they cared for their animals, how they landscaped their yards, even how they dressed.

I even managed to whip out a "That is such a pretty sweater—I wish I had your fashion sense." (And, to my surprise, the nice lady took it well.)

Then I went to the grocery store.

And let's just say that no one in a grocery store expects you to walk by and compliment them—not even the people who work there.

And let's just say that "Wow, you picked the perfect melon" isn't the right way to go.

And neither is "You look like you're on a mission. You seem extremely well organized."

And "I wish I was as good at choosing the right steaks as you are" falls pretty flat.

And let's just say I wanted to give up. In some settings, it seemed, compliments are not just unexpected but also unwanted.

Still, I decided to try one more time, but with a twist. I decided to ask for help, because asking for help is implicitly complimentary. If I ask you for help, I'm saying you know something I don't know or you can do something I can't do. Asking for help is like saying, "I respect your (knowledge/skill/experience)."

That's what I did. I was in the seafood section and made eye contact with a thirtysomething woman. She didn't smile or nod (gulp!) but I forged ahead.

"I'm terrible at picking the right piece of salmon," I said. "Can I bother you for a second and ask you to help me?" And she did. In fact, she appeared to enjoy it.

And I got to say, "I really appreciate it. Thanks for helping me, and for being so nice."

So while I did experience a couple of tough moments—especially when I found myself standing in the checkout line behind an extremely frazzled father with three borderline-out-of-control kids and the last thing he seemed to want was a random compliment—I made it out of the grocery store and out of the parking lot with my compliment streak intact.

But I do have to admit I was relieved to get back in the car.

My Evening

And then relief turned to panic when I went to the gym.

On one hand, it was easier: Most people wear headphones when they work out, so that eliminated them from my challenge.

On the other hand, moving from bench to machines to free weights meant that I ran into almost everyone who was at the gym.

Still. One guy was benching 325 pounds, for reps. Easy compliment. A woman was doing a split and then laying her torso all the way forward onto the mat. Another easy compliment. A guy jumped in and helped an apparent newcomer with his form on squats; presumptuous, yes, but also kind, because the way the guy was bending his back was a recipe for injury. When I ran into the Good Samaritan a few minutes later, it was easy for me to say, "That was really nice of you to help him out."

Then I found myself doing pull-downs near a guy doing seated rows. And I had nothing . . . until I noticed the tattoo on his forearm.

And I was in. "I really like your tattoo," I said.

He smiled, said thanks, and then spent the next five minutes talking all about it: where he got it, how he came up with the design, what it meant to him . . . I realized that sometimes the easiest thing to compliment is the thing that people seem to want you to notice, or are obviously proud of: a tattoo, a piercing, an unusual hair color, a Porsche, a Hayabusa, a tricked-out truck . . . Almost everyone has something they do or say or wear that they feel represents who they are inside.

All you need to do is look for it.

My Takeaways

I can't say it was easy. Complimenting every single person I ran into got easier, but never *easy*. It's not hard to compliment people you meet who are doing their jobs: grocery clerks, managers, front-desk people at the gym . . . Saying thanks and telling them they did something well is not difficult at all.

All that's required is that you remember to actually *do* it.

Complimenting "random" people is harder but surprisingly rewarding. It was fun to watch people's faces light up.

Try it. You'll think so too. Every day, people around you do good things. Most of those people don't work for you; in fact, most of them have no relationship with you, professional or personal. Compliment them for something they would least expect.

Expected feels good.

Unexpected makes an even bigger impact.

Don't just take my word for it.

Complimenting people who try something different can also be hard. Do it anyway. Status quo is often status safe. Taking a risk, however small, is hard, especially if you're insecure. Insecurity feeds off silence, so mention when you see someone trying something different. Compliment the effort. Praise the risk.

Even if what they have tried doesn't work, they will know you noticed. Everyone likes to be noticed. And they'll know, regardless of how it turns out, that you respect them for trying.

Most of all, make the compliment personal. Compliment what the person did to achieve a certain outcome, not the outcome itself.

And never be afraid to ask for help, because the act of asking is a compliment in itself—and it gives you the chance to praise that person for his or her knowledge and skill.

Give it a try. Make tomorrow an Extreme Productivity Day where you work your number, and make that number praise. Commit to complimenting five people, or ten, or even everyone you meet.

Other people will appreciate it. Research shows that more people leave a job due to a lack of recognition than for any other reason. Statistics show that children are happier, more motivated, and more successful when they receive regular encouragement and specific praise. And no science is needed to know that the faces of your family and friends light up when you compliment them.

Then you can use that gratification and fulfillment to motivate you to try the next strategy, because while it works, it is definitely not easy.

Why? Because you'll need to *do what the pros do*.

CHAPTER 7

You Don't Need a Coach; You Need a Pro

Three quarters of Americans say they regularly experience physiological and psychological symptoms caused by stress. Research shows that Generation Z in particular is much less able to manage and deal with stress: Feelings of fear, trepidation, and hesitance keep them from performing as well as they could. A lunch with NASCAR driver Joey Logano might fix that for them. It did for me.

Joey? Joey loves pressure.

In fact, Joey thinks pressure is a privilege.

"I don't think about ways I can screw this up or how this might be my only shot," he told me. "It's not going to be my only shot. I'm only twenty-six. I have time left. I will work hard to make sure I get more moments like this. I love having that do-or-die moment."

Do what the pros do: Find a person who challenges you. Find a person who lays out a process so seemingly daunting, so seemingly insurmountable, a course wherein the *there* seems insurmountable but so does the *here* . . . and who helps you achieve something you never dreamed you could.

By now you might be tired of hearing me talk about Jeremiah Bishop and the time I rode his Gran Fondo. You might be, but I'm not. Jeremiah helped me accomplish something incredibly hard and gave me the confidence to try other extremely challenging things. How did I download as much of his expertise onto my mental hard drive as possible?

THAT SINKING FEELING MEANS YOU'RE ON THE RIGHT TRACK

You know the sensation. The sinking feeling you get in the pit of your stomach when an idea initially sounded great but now the cold, stark, horrifying reality has set in.

I do. Big time.

I wanted to tackle a huge goal. I wanted to find a person to help me achieve something that felt impossible, at least for me.

So I called Jeremiah.

Jeremiah Bishop is basically to mountain bike racing what an NBA All-Star is to basketball. For years, he has been one of the most versatile and accomplished riders in the world. He's won the Pan American Games, did the double in 2008 by winning the

U.S. Short Track Cross Country and the Marathon Mountain Bike National Championships, and was a twelve-time member of the U.S. national team.

I told him I was looking for a nearly impossible (at least for me) physical challenge. Maybe I could train for and ride a mass-participation event, or possibly complete in a certain time a route he devised for me, or what else? I didn't know. I had recently started riding a road bike to try to get in better shape, and aside from seeking a challenge that involved cycling, I didn't have any real ideas.

But he did: Ride his inaugural Alpine Loop Gran Fondo.

At first, the idea didn't seem too bad; 107 miles sounded long but, at least in theory, manageable. Serious cycling enthusiasts routinely complete "century rides" of 100 miles or more.

Except that even for serious enthusiasts, his event was savage. The route followed his favorite hard-core training ride and included paved climbs over two mountains plus dirt-road climbs over two more mountains. (One climb used a dirt/gravel fire access road that crests Reddish Knob, at 4,400 feet one of the highest points in Virginia.)

As Jeremiah told me, "Think of it like completing a marathon, as long as that marathon also involves running up and over a mountain." Daunting enough for a guy who had been riding a bike for less than a month, but it got better (or worse, depending on your perspective): I had a little over three months to get ready.

And that's how that sinking feeling in my stomach soon became my new best friend.

Because he had agreed to be my pro, the first step was to take a ride with Jeremiah so he could evaluate my fitness and form.

We rode a few miles before Jeremiah chose a short but relatively steep hill to gauge my current level of fitness. Within moments my heart rate had soared to 160 beats per minute, flirted briefly with the 170s, and finally settled firmly into the 180s. (Because in theory my maximum heart rate should have been no more than 170 or so, 184 beats per minute was what exercise physiologists generally call "high.")

My vision tunneled. I felt that nauseous and woozy "I'm about to faint and that's actually cool with me because lying on the ground sounds really, really appealing" feeling. Before I did, though, fatigue made a coward out of me, as fatigue is wont to do . . . and I stopped about thirty feet from the top of the hill.

I sagged over my handlebars and managed to glance sideways at Jeremiah's heart rate monitor.

It read 125 beats per minute.

At that moment I learned three more things:

1. Having a pro also means your pro is a (freaking) pro.
2. When you think your pro is speaking to you, he may actually be narrating the video he's recording of your near-death state.

3. Your pro can get you to where you want to go because he won't coddle you or tell you what you want to hear; he'll tell you what you *need* to hear and *need* to do.

That's because your pro will often simply lay out what other highly successful people did to achieve that level of success—people you will never meet. For example, Stephen King writes two thousand words a day and, as he says in his book *On Writing: A Memoir of the Craft,* "only under dire circumstances" will he allow himself to shut down before he gets his two thousand words. (Yep, the Kingster works his number.) If you want to be a writer, you could do a lot worse than simply doing what *that* pro does.

That's why you don't need a coach. You don't need someone to encourage you, to coddle you to adapt their knowledge and skills and expertise to your capabilities. . . . You need someone to say, "This is how I do it," and then let you do it.

Coaches coach, and they're great if that's what you want. But if you want to accomplish what the pros have accomplished, you don't need a coach. You need a pro. All you have to do is choose people who have accomplished things that you wish to accomplish and follow their leads.

The blueprint is there. If you're into fitness, workout plans abound. If you're into business, biographies abound. If you want to learn a particular skill, the blueprints are there. Just be willing to follow them. Don't think you can somehow "hack" your way to the same level of success. You aren't that smart. I'm not that smart. Maybe Tim Ferriss is that smart, but there's only one Tim Ferriss. Ask him. He'll tell you.

(Just playing, Tim.)

So no, you don't need to know the pro you emulate.

HOW TO PICK YOUR PRO

Whom you choose to admire—and it is a choice—says more about you than about that person. We tend to admire certain people because we see something of ourselves in them. We like to think that what they do and how they do it indicates what we would do if given the chance.

Say you're a tech entrepreneur. You may admire Mark Zuckerberg for staying the course and reportedly turning down a $1 billion offer from Yahoo!, or you may admire Mark Cuban because he cashed out by selling Broadcast.com to Yahoo! for more than $5 billion just a few years after cofounding the company.

Maybe your hero is Sara Blakely, the founder of Spanx, who—and this is even more difficult—is raising four children. Maybe you admire Sheryl Sandberg because she's a successful businesswoman or because she works tirelessly to help women (and men) find ways to lead more fulfilling and successful lives. (Or maybe you admire her for both reasons.)

Maybe your hero is Richard Branson; if you were a billionaire, you would be an adventure-seeking, publicity-generating machine too.

(But keep in mind that for Branson, experiencing adventure was the primary purpose. "It was the adventure that was irresistible, basically," he told me, "but there was the by-product that Virgin as a brand became an adventurous brand, a sexy brand, and I think some of these adventures did actually help with that. Today Virgin is one of the better-known brands in the world. It punches quite a long way above its weight compared with its turnover and profits. I had a lot of fun, incredible adventures, and the by-product from a branding point of view was positive as well.")

Or maybe you'd take an opposite approach and choose Brad Kelley as your hero. If you were a billionaire who owned more land than the area of Rhode Island, you would make sure no one has heard of you either.

It doesn't matter whom you admire. It doesn't matter whom you look to for inspiration; you're seeking more of a blueprint for success. Whom you choose is important only in that their approach to success will help you achieve your goals.

You can even take a counterintuitive approach and think well outside the hero box. Think of someone who is extremely successful but whom you would normally never dream of emulating.

If you're shy and reserved, pick a relentless self-promoter. If you love shooting from the hip, pick someone known for thorough analysis. If you always seek to build consensus through compromise, pick someone who often takes a bold stand.

Then pick a specific skill, quality, or attribute, and do something the way that person would do it. It won't be comfortable. It won't feel natural. But it will stretch you and take you to places you otherwise never would have gone.

And then, if what you've done so far hasn't taken you where you want to go, take a bigger swing at the emulation target. Learn as much as you can about that person and adopt as many of their habits and routines as you possibly can.

THE DIFFERENCE BETWEEN PROS AND MOTIVATIONAL COACHES

My first week of cycling training, my pro was in Italy racing in the UCI Mountain Bike Marathon World Championships.

Granted, my situation was different because Jeremiah is a professional athlete. But the average cycling coach works with athletes from afar, e-mailing training plans, reviewing training logs, checking in remotely, etc.

In fact, cycling coaches are emblematic of the sport and of life. Responsibility rests squarely on the cyclist, not the coach. Cycling coaches advise, mentor, and motivate but, like a supervisor overseeing remote teams or a business owner managing multiple locations, they cannot and do not directly supervise or enforce.

And my pro had zero interest in supervising me even if he did have the time. That's one of the reasons he excels in his sport: From his perspective, anyone who states a goal must naturally be willing to do whatever it takes to achieve that goal.

That's why there are coaches . . . and there are pros. Coaches think about making the process fun and uplifting. Pros show you how to succeed—and expect you to take full responsibility for your own success.

Pros will help you stop believing that making a few small tweaks will somehow change your life. Pros will help you stop believing that you can just do a little bit more of what you have always done and somehow that minor change will make all the difference. I stopped trying to just think positively. I stopped setting only reachable goals. I stopped thinking I could somehow "hack" my way to success. I didn't do all the stuff we're told to do . . . because all the stuff we're told to do never, ever works.

Take a different approach. Ask someone who has been there and done that—a real pro—what they would do in your shoes.

And then *do* what they tell you to do, because unlike most people, however well-meaning they may be, a pro *knows*.

"I can't believe I did that"·is incredibly powerful. You start to crave that feeling. You start to crave the suffering (whether physical or mental) because you crave that feeling of accomplishment when you finish the day's routine. You look forward to the "pain" because it is followed by the joy of success.

And in time, while you may never be as accomplished as the pro you emulate, you will be a member of the club. You will become a cyclist ... or a runner ... or a leader ... or an entrepreneur ... or a philanthropist . . . or whatever it is you set out to be.

And that feels amazing too, because when you've become something, you need almost no motivation at all in order to keep being what you have become.

It's no longer what you do. It's what you *are*.

HOW TO CONNECT WITH YOUR PRO

Some people prefer not to emulate from afar. Some prefer direct contact and the sense of connection it imparts. That approach means finding a pro who will work with or mentor you.

The process starts with finding a way to fit in with the community you hope to join: leaders, parents, entrepreneurs, fitness enthusiasts, etc.

Fortunately, that's a natural urge. We all want to feel like we're part of a community or that we're part of something larger than ourselves.

But if you're like me, fitting in is not so easy. For one thing, I'm shy. I'm fairly introverted in informal group settings. (Though I don't mind speaking to crowds at all—as many introverts know, that's different.) I'm hardly brimming with natural self-confidence (unless I'm in the right setting; as it is with many people, my self-confidence is largely situational).

So when I realized being cycling-scrawny (six feet tall, 150 pounds) is great for road cycling but is far from the healthiest of looks, I joined a gym. I started lifting weights. I felt like a fish totally out of water. Any upper-body strength I'd once had was long gone. No one was lifting less weight than I was.

I hated it. I felt like whoever looked at me was judging me. Not that many people were looking. Most—especially the big boys—brushed past me as if I weren't there.

But I stuck with it and got a little stronger. I got a little bigger. In time I was able to lift more weight for more reps and more sets. That helped me get a little stronger and a little bigger too. (That's how it works.)

One day an archetype of a gym rat—shaved head, cut-off shirt, veins like ropes in his arms—was doing side-to-side pull-ups: hands close together, looking along the bar rather than facing it, pulling up and alternating bringing his head above the bar on the right side and then the left. I was looking for different exercises to do and I'm not sure what possessed me, but when he finished his set, I said, "I've never seen pull-ups done that way. Where are you feeling them?"

As soon as the words were out of my mouth, I thought, "Oh, great. He's going to blow me off."

Instead, he smiled. "Yeah, those are really hard," he said. "I definitely feel them in my lats, but I like how it brings my core into it. You should try them."

I said thanks and started to walk away.

"Hey," he said, "I've noticed you often change the width of your grip when you do dips. Why is that?"

In that moment several things flashed through my mind. One, I was surprised he'd even noticed how I did dips. Two, I was shocked he was asking *me* for advice. And three, in an environment where I had always felt a little uncomfortable and a lot insecure, I was evidently starting to fit in.

And cheesy as it might sound, that felt really good. Twenty-five pounds with no increase in body-fat percentage later, I no longer feel like I don't fit in.

I'm far from the biggest or strongest, and that was never my goal. But it is really nice to exchange hellos, to exchange nods, to ask questions or give a little advice. I've become a member of a small community of people with a shared interest and a shared purpose.

Fitting in feels good, even somewhere relatively meaningless and insignificant like a small-town gym.

So how can you fit in when you don't feel you belong, whether in a group, an organization, or even a workplace?

It just takes the right approach:

Start Quietly and Just Do the Work

We've all been in situations where "that guy" (it's always a guy) shows up for the first time and immediately tries to force his way into a group.

Don't be that guy.

Say you join an industry organization. Show up for every meeting. Contribute in small ways but otherwise lie low. Show that you recognize you're new. Show that you don't expect to be taken seriously until you prove you're serious—and are in it for the long haul.

Volunteer for the Worst Jobs

"That guy" tries to leapfrog his way to the plum tasks. Sometimes he even manages to pull it off, but the cost, in terms of belonging, is high.

Instead, use the time you're lying low to figure out where you can make the biggest difference to the people in the group. Hint: Just find ways to make their lives easier. Volunteer for the grunt work. Volunteer for the glory-free tasks. Volunteer to pay your dues.

Ask for Help That Requires Only Words

"That guy" goes to a networking event and, moments after meeting you, wants an introduction to someone you know, or wants you to wrangle him an appointment with one of your customers, or wants you to—well, you know how it goes. We all need help. We all need assistance. But once you've paid some dues, be smart and start small. Don't ask for time or effort. Just ask a question.

Offer to Help in Ways That Require More Than Words

"That guy" immediately walks over and tells you what you're doing wrong. Or what you could be doing better. Or could be doing differently. Or, most likely, what you should be doing his way.

That kind of help is more about "that guy" than about you— much less about what you may actually need.

Pay attention so you'll notice when other people are struggling. Then come up with specific ways to help—that way you can push past the automatic "No, I'm okay" responses.

Very few people offer help before they have been asked, even though most of the time that is when a little help will make the greatest impact. Just make sure you offer to roll up your sleeves and really help—that's the only way to make a real difference in another person's life.

Help Other People Feel They Belong

Think of it this way. No matter how welcoming and new-employee-friendly the company, recently hired employees often feel they're constantly being weighed, measured, and found wanting.

Maybe it's the guy in shipping who always eats lunch alone. Maybe it's the lady in accounting who always stands at the edge of a group. It's easy to spot people who feel hesitant and out of place.

Pick one. Say hi. Say something nice. Say, or do, something that makes the person feel a slightly bigger connection—to the company, to a group, or just to you.

Reach the point at which you feel confident helping others fit in and that's when *you* truly fit in—because then it's no longer about you: It's about the group and the people in that group.

Which, when you think about it, is the perfect definition of fitting in.

And which, when you think even harder about it, is the perfect time to ask someone you admire how they gained the skill or expertise they possess—and how you can too.

I promise they won't ignore your request, because you've proven yourself as someone who helps others . . . which means people will gladly help you.

Who you look to for inspiration is important, but what really matters is that their approach to success will help you achieve your goals.

And that their success—and their approach to achieving that success—will serve as an example to help you overcome your self-imposed limits.

YOUR BIGGEST LIMITS ARE SELF-IMPOSED—BUT THOSE LIMITS ARE THE EASIEST TO OVERCOME

Granted, we all have limits. Some limits are physical. Some are mental. Some we simply can't do anything about.

But in most cases, our limits are self-imposed.

Here's an example of a self-imposed limit: effort. It's easy to rationalize that we've done enough. It's tempting to think we've done all we can, especially when we're tired. And so we stop.

But that little voice lies: With the right motivation, or under the right circumstances, we can always do more. Stopping is nearly always a choice. We don't have to stop; we choose to stop.

The same is true for skill. Once you reach a certain level of expertise, your rate of improvement typically slows . . . and it's natural to assume you're near your limit.

But you really aren't. You just think so because you've started comparing your present self with your past self instead of with what is actually possible. You've started to look back at how far you've come instead of looking forward to see just how far you can still go. You assume you're as good as you're likely to ever be.

And so, often unconsciously, you stop trying.

Here's a great example.

Last year I went to a go-kart track with some NASCAR executives and three actual racers: Alon Day, EuroNASCAR series driver and 2016 Israeli Athlete of the Year; Ty Majeski, 2016 ARCA Midwest Tour champion; and Ross Chastain, Xfinity Series driver, occasional truck series driver, and all-around good guy.

I've been to kart tracks before and typically finish well compared with other weekend warriors. But against three professional drivers? On the very first practice lap they all flashed past me going into a series of *S* turns.

I knew they would be fast, but their speed seemed surreal. I couldn't imagine ever going that fast.

But I settled in and tried to find the best lines, the best braking points—practice is all about experimenting. I did my best and finished the practice session with the fifth-quickest time out of ten people.

I was about half a second behind a nonracer. Not bad. Except Alon, Ty, and Ross were nearly five seconds faster.

Ugh.

While we took a break, the other nonracers chatted with one another. I went straight to Ross and asked him how he was so quick.

He looked out at the track for a moment. "Were you flat out through the *S*'s?" he asked.

"Um, no," I said, narrowing my eyes with skepticism. Pedal

to the metal on a tight track might seem fast, but it's usually not. In some places on a track, you have to go slow in order to be fast. "I didn't think I could."

"Sure you can," he said. "Go in wide, tap the inside corner of the first turn, then tap the wall just before the narrowest point on the next one. That's the line you want to take. The back end might slide a little on the exit of the last turn and you may kiss the wall, but that's okay."

"'Okay'?" I thought. "Easy for your NASCAR-driver ass to say."

Oddly enough, though, it was easy for my skeptical ass to actually do. On my first qualifying lap, I used the line he recommended and entered the first S turn flat out . . . and never had to lift off the throttle. That alone made me much faster because I carried extra speed into the straightaway and through the following right-hand sweeper.

What changed? My skill wasn't the problem. My self-imposed limit was the problem. I didn't think it was possible to go flat out . . . so it wasn't. Once I knew it was possible, it was possible.

Nothing changed except my perspective—and, as a result, my skill.

I had stopped thinking about going a little faster than I had earlier and started thinking about trying to be as fast as Ross. I was no longer my benchmark. Ross was my benchmark.

After qualifying—and using a few other tips Ross gave me

about a few other turns—I was fourth fastest behind Alon, Ross, and Ty. With a little more practice, their lap times had improved by about half a second more than the practice session.

My lap times had improved by more than three seconds.

For the race, we lined up in qualifying order, ten feet separating each kart. As the laps wound down, Alon, Ross, and Ty gradually eased into the distance. I did manage to lap all but one of the other karts and kept from being lapped by the fast guys.

But for the most part I just tried to race the track and drive the way Ross would. Of course I couldn't—but I tried, because he was my benchmark.

And that mental shift made me faster: My fastest lap was almost a second quicker than my best qualifying lap because I forgot my self-imposed limits and instead focused on trying to achieve what was actually possible.

And you can do the same.

Stop comparing yourself with yourself. Stop comparing yourself with the people around you. Go see a superstar in action. Whether it's a speaker, a musician, a performer, an athlete, or an entrepreneur, find a way to expose yourself to exceptional skill, exceptional expertise, and exceptional talent.

I've ridden with professional cyclists; the experience, while humbling, automatically ratcheted my performance bar higher. I've worked with one of the queens of data analysis; the experience, while humbling, automatically ratcheted my own problem-solving expectations much higher.

When you spend time with a superstar, when you try to do what the pros do, that experience will automatically ratchet your own internal limits to a higher level. While you may never be as good, when superstar performance is your bar, you automatically set your goals higher—and that makes you achieve more. Stop comparing your present self with your past self.

Start comparing your present self—regardless of how far you think you have already come—with what is actually possible.

Stop looking back. Start looking forward to see how far you can still go.

And then work hard to get there. Do what the pros do.

You may never be as talented as the absolute best in the field or pursuit you choose, but you will definitely achieve much more than your self-imposed limits allowed you to think was ever possible.

TO ACCOMPLISH A HUGE GOAL, GO VIKING

Clive Standen is the actor who plays Rollo on *Vikings* and Bryan Mills on the NBC show *Taken*. Because of *Vikings* he may seem like an overnight success, but he had been an actor for many years before getting that role. How did he hang in there during the lean times?

"I'm a husband and the father of three kids," he told me. "I have the pressure of putting food on the table. The cliché is that when you have kids you stop worrying about yourself, but you really do. Becoming a parent changed everything for me.

"When things aren't going so well, you simply do whatever it takes. When I was struggling, I had no pride in terms of what jobs I would take: I drove vans, passed out things on the street, waited tables, did bar work, cleaned houses. . . . The mortgage doesn't pay itself. That was motivation enough.

"On the flip side, having kids gives you less time to devote to putting food on the table. When you have kids, you think you'll have less time, but I actually find more time. We waste so many hours in the day procrastinating. Nowadays those hours when the kids are at school are the ones that I make sure I use to get the work done. (I don't want to take away from time with the kids.) I don't waste it; I use that time. I find myself getting far more done as a parent because I seize those opportunities. Ultimately, I do everything for my family. Even if means staying up all night, you make the time."

If you're struggling to manage your time effectively, Clive's is the perfect approach. Decide what is important to you and then structure your life—and your process—to ensure you accomplish the things that really matter.

"As for 'hanging in there,' as you put it," Clive continues, "Richard Briers came to our drama school and we asked him a similar question. 'How do you hang in there? How do you get through the hard times?'

"He said, 'If you really, really, really, really, really, really, really, really, really, *really* want to act, don't. But if you *have* to act, then do it.'

"It's not as easy as saying, 'Well, it's not working out, so what else am I good at?' That's another motivation for me. There is nothing else I am as good at as acting that satisfies that hunger as much.

"So I didn't have a choice. I *had* to hang in there."

Do you have a choice? If your goal means enough to you, then you don't. Act that way. Hanging in there and staying the course will help fuel your motivation to continue.

But what if you lack confidence? What if that's holding you back? Emulate someone like Tamara Taylor, an actress on *Bones*. As a child, Tamara was painfully shy. What did she do about it? She decided to try acting in order to overcome her fear. Although as you'll see, "overcome" is the wrong word because, as for many of us, confidence isn't just a switch for Tamara that, once flipped, stays on forever.

Confidence is earned each and every day . . . and the process often starts when you dive in and do what you're most afraid to do.

"I know it sounds crazy, but it made sense for me," Tamara told me. "One, I love—*love*—movies, and that still, quiet part of myself thought I might be good at acting if I tried it. But that was also the thing that scared me the most. I was so shy it almost paralyzed me in social settings. And as shy people know, that can become a vicious cycle: The more uncomfortable you feel around people, the more you retreat, and the more shy you get.

"Fortunately, my best friend in the world had moved to Los Angeles and gotten a part on a hit TV show, and I thought, 'If only I could do that . . .' So I got into an acting class because it scared me to my core.

"The glorious surprise was I actually loved acting. It took many years of acting classes to get even remotely comfortable, but that's okay. It helped me so much on a personal level, not to mention professionally."

Tamara also has an awesome perspective on staying the course and how even the smallest successes helped fuel her motivation.

"The key to my perseverance was absolutely loving the craft of acting," she said. "I just figured that if I kept doing it, at the very least I would get better at acting. Even if I didn't become a tremendous success, so long as I knew I was improving and getting better, to me, *that* was success. Feeling successful is internal, not external.

"There's that Steve Jobs quote that says the people who are crazy enough to think they can change the world are the ones who do . . . and it does require a little bit of 'crazy' to say the light is green when the world is telling you the light is red. The world tells lots of people the light is red. You have to trust yourself and say, 'I think the light is green, and I'm going to keep doing this.' As long as you keep going, you'll keep getting better. And as you get better, you gain more confidence. That alone to me is success."

See? It's easy to find pros to emulate. What is harder is committing to do what the pros do—but it's not nearly so hard when you realize how well it works. Embrace the challenge, embrace the "pain," embrace the fact that you will stretch and push yourself beyond your normal limits . . . because every time you do, you'll feel motivated to do it again.

And in time you'll find yourself living the life *you* want to live.

CHAPTER 8

Do More by Doing Less

We've talked a lot about success. We've talked a lot about achievement. We've looked at plenty of examples of extremely accomplished, often even famous, people and how they achieved that success.

They're great.

We all dream of being great . . . but we can't all be great at everything.

But we can be the best we can be at the things we choose to do.

That's how every successful person starts out. They don't *know* they'll be superstars. They don't know they'll be world-class. They just know they want to be as good as they can be.

BE THE BIGGEST FISH

Say you're speaking at an event. Your goal is to be the best speaker at *that* event. You don't have to be as good as Tony Robbins, who, for all the fun I poke at him, is a tremendous speaker. You just need to be the best speaker at that event. You need to stand out from the other speakers. You need to be special in some way: funnier, smarter, more enthusiastic, more insightful . . . you need to be the person at that event who provides the best value to the audience.

Then people will remember you. Then people will check out your other work. Then other conferences will want to book you. Being the best naturally creates greater opportunities.

Or say you attend a meeting. Your goal isn't to be the Stephen Covey of meetings; your goal is to be the most prepared, or the most on point, or the most knowledgeable, or the most engaged. Your goal is to be the best person attending *that* meeting.

Or say you work in customer service. While you ultimately may want to prove that you have the potential to hold higher-level positions, your immediate goal is to be the best in your company at what you *currently* do or, barring that, to be the best at some aspect of your job.

That's how you stand out. That's how you get noticed. That's how you move up the ladder of achievement.

That's how you get the skills, expertise, and experience you might not gain if you settle for being average. And that's also how you become part of a community . . . and become who you want to be.

This "be the best" principle can be applied anywhere.

Take me. I sometimes go on rides with local riders who are not only younger but also professional cyclists. (Add that to the list of ways it sucks to be me.) When I'm riding with the fast guys, I will never be the best cyclist.

But I can be the most helpful person on the ride. I can be the guy who takes the longest lead-outs into a headwind. Or I can be the guy who always brings extra tubes and CO_2 cartridges in case someone else has a flat and didn't bring theirs. Or I can be the best "he's pretty slow but he's entertaining to have along" guy.

So that's what I do. I find some way to be the best. It's more fun for me and for the people I ride with. I've become a better cyclist just by riding with the fast guys.

And I feel welcomed in a setting where I otherwise would never feel I belonged.

We all have our sweet spot—yet most of us spend a fraction of our day actually working in our sweet spots. The key is to find ways to delegate or streamline all the tasks that distract you from doing what you do best, because when you do more of what you do best, you achieve more—and your career or your business or your personal life naturally flourishes.

How can you free up time so you can apply other achievement strategies to the things you do best, and learn to perform those things even better than you already do?

That's hard, because if you're already somewhat successful, success tends to create clutter: more meetings, more projects, more decisions, more items on your to-do list. But often doing more can mean achieving less.

That's why, once again, subtraction can be the best addition, especially when you streamline your day and, in the process, your life.

And the easiest way to do that is to start saying no.

THE ANTIDRUG COMMERCIALS ARE RIGHT: JUST SAY NO

As an employee, as a business owner, as a parent or friend, you constantly say yes: to opportunities, to ideas, to things you can do to help other people and make a difference in their lives . . . Saying yes is a crucial element in your success.

But so is saying no.

In fact, if you want to achieve a huge goal, as well as succeed at all your other responsibilities, you need to learn how to say no to most things that come your way. Otherwise other people—and other choices—will place incredible demands on your most valuable resource: your time.

Ryan Robinson, a serial entrepreneur and marketer, uses a simple framework for deciding whether to say yes or no. He asks himself two questions:

"Will Doing This Benefit Me in Some Way?"

Of course, "benefits" come in many forms. Benefits may be financial. Benefits may be professional. Benefits may be in the form of greater fulfillment, greater satisfaction, the joy of doing good. Just as the definition of "success" is unique to each person, so is the definition of "benefits."

That means only you can decide whether a certain opportunity, activity, or request benefits you.

Say you're asked to speak at an event. That may be a cool opportunity, but what if the only benefit to you involves your ego? If you have nothing better to do, go for it . . . but shouldn't you use that time to do more of what you do best?

Or say you could throw your name in the hat to serve on your company's employee picnic team. (Yes, those do exist.) That may be a cool opportunity, but then again, probably not—your time would be better spent focused on areas that drive real value for your organization. No matter what your business, one or two things truly drive results. Maybe it's quality. Maybe it's service. Maybe it's being the lowest-cost provider. Maybe it's the personal connection made with each individual customer. Other aspects are important, but for every business, one or two are absolutely make-or-break. Want to succeed? Spend all the time you can working on the area that drives real value for your business. *That's* how you'll stand out. *That's* what you should do best—and do more of.

Ruthlessly evaluate every "opportunity" that comes your way. Remember, every time you say yes, you take time away from doing what you do best.

Make sure that "yes" is genuinely worth it.

"Is This More Important Than What I'm Currently Doing?"

Now the rubber meets the road.

You already have nonnegotiable goals: meeting your basic financial needs, meeting your basic health needs, taking care of your family . . . If the "opportunity" negatively impacts those things, boom: automatic "no."

But what about your negotiable goals? Here it gets stickier— but not really. Which is more important to you: the "opportunity" or what you are currently working to achieve?

The answer is always easier than you think. If you decided to, say, run a marathon, and you've been working hard and following your routine, there's no reason to switch fitness goals in midstream. You'll achieve your goal of running a marathon, and then you can put on your serial-achiever hat and achieve a different goal—and you'll bring the confidence and motivation you've gained from achieving your marathon goal to your next pursuit.

All you have to do is balance what you're currently doing

against what you could do. Which is more important? Which will lead you to the success you hope to achieve? Which will make you feel happier and more fulfilled? Which will better ensure that your "financial" and "happiness" graph lines intersect?

Most of the time you'll find that what you're currently doing is more important. Don't grab every new shiny thing in the hope that it will somehow make you happier.

That will help you with future time wasters, but what about the time sucks you currently deal with?

Let's eliminate some of those.

TO ACHIEVE A LOT MORE, START BY DOING A LOT LESS

Instead of doing a total professional or personal makeover, the easiest way is to start small. Here are some basic things to eliminate that will free up chunks of time to allow you to spend more of your time doing what you do best.

Eliminate One "Permission"

You probably don't think of it this way, but everything you do "trains" the people around you to treat you a certain way. Let employees interrupt your meetings or phone calls because of "emergencies," and they'll feel free to interrupt you whenever they want. Drop what you're doing every time a friend calls, and that person will always expect immediate attention. Return e-mails immediately, and people will learn to expect an immediate response.

In short, your actions give other people permission to keep you from functioning the way you function best.

How do you change that paradigm? A friend created an "emergency" e-mail account. He responds to those e-mails immediately. His employees know he checks his "standard" e-mail only a couple times a day. They act accordingly. Unless his wife is calling, a stay-at-home dad I know answers his phone only when his kids are napping. People know he's not always available and they act accordingly.

Figure out how you operate best and then "train" the people around you to let you be as productive as you possibly can.

Kill One Report

You're not reading most of them anyway. And neither are other people.

Kill One Sign-off

I worked at a manufacturing plant where supervisors had to sign off on quality before a job could be run. That seemed strange to me: We trusted the operators to ensure that jobs met standards throughout the run, so why couldn't we trust them to know if a job met quality standards before they started running?

You probably have at least one sign-off in place because somewhere along the way an employee made a major error and you don't want the same mistake to happen again. In the process, though, you decrease the degree of responsibility your employees feel for their own work, because your authority has been inserted into the process.

Do this instead: Train, explain, trust . . . and remove yourself from processes where you don't belong.

That also works where kids are concerned. Set guidelines and then allow your kids to make decisions within those parameters. They'll learn to be more responsible and independent, and you'll regain all that time you spend (fruitlessly) micromanaging their lives.

Fire One Customer

You know the one: The high maintenance, low revenue, nonexistent profits one. Start charging more or providing less. If that's not possible, fire that customer.

That's also true for your "friends," by the way. Some people are all take and no give. Some people suck time and energy that you can't afford to lose. As Jim Rohn says, you are the average of the five people you spend the most time with. There's nothing wrong with firing a few "friends," especially if they aren't really friends.

Prune Your To-Do List

Earlier we discussed how a twenty- or thirty-item to-do list is just a wish list. A twenty- or thirty-item to-do list is not just depressing, it's impossible. Why start when there's no way you can finish? You don't—and you don't.

Try this instead. Create an actual wish list. Write down all the ideas, projects, tasks, etc. you can think of. Make it a "would like to do" list.

Then choose the three or four items from that list that will make the biggest difference. Pick the easiest tasks to accomplish, or the ones with the biggest payoff, or the ones that will eliminate the most pain. Make *that* your to-do list. Get it done.

Then you can go back and choose three or four more items from your wish list.

Cut One Expense

Currently you're spending money on something you don't need or don't want. But because you buy it, you feel you must use it. I used to subscribe to a variety of magazines (because subscribing is cheap compared with purchasing magazines at the newsstand). Great . . . but then the magazines appeared in my mailbox. And then I felt I must read them. When I didn't, they sat around and made me feel guilty.

So I dropped most of them. I don't miss them.

Often the biggest savings when you cut an expense don't involve the actual cost; the biggest savings lie in the time involved in doing or maintaining or consuming whatever the expense represents. Pick one expense you can eliminate that will also free up time and effort. And you'll get to do more of what you do best.

Drop One Personal Commitment

We all do things simply because we feel we should. Maybe you volunteer because a friend asked you to . . . but you feel no real connection to the cause you support. Maybe you have a weekly lunch with some old friends . . . but it feels more like a chore than a treat. Or maybe you keep trying to learn French just because you started . . . and now you don't want to feel like a quitter.

Think about one thing you do out of habit, or because you think you're supposed to, or simply because you don't know how to get out of it—and then find a way to get out of it. The momentary pain—or in some cases confrontation—of stepping down, dropping out, or letting go will be soon be replaced by a huge sense of relief.

Then use that time to do something with real meaning.

Streamline Your Lunch

You already make enough decisions. What to have for lunch shouldn't be one of them. Do as I do and eat tuna and a small salad. Pick something healthy, something simple.

Save the decision making for the things that are genuinely important.

As a bonus, you'll lose a little weight and feel a little better.

Create a Window of Reflection

Most people spend a lot more time reacting—to employees and colleagues, to customer requests, to the needs of family and friends, etc.—than they do thinking and reflecting. Eliminate twenty to thirty minutes of reacting time by creating some quiet time. Close your door and think. Better yet, go for a walk. Exercise does more to bolster thinking than thinking does; walking just forty minutes three days a week builds new brain cells and improves your memory function.

And don't worry that something bad will happen while you're gone—most of the time, the issues you "avoid" will solve themselves.

Eliminate an Entire Category of Decisions

Instead of making serial decisions, try making just one: Decide who will decide.

Say you regularly need to decide whether to expedite shipping due to work-in-progress delays. Instead of being the go-to decision maker, pick someone else in the organization to make those decisions. Provide guidance, parameters, and advice, and turn that person loose. Then check in periodically to see if they need more direction. That way you get to spend time figuring out how to eliminate the delays instead of dealing with the repercussions.

Almost every decision you currently make can be taken over by people you trust. How will you learn to trust them? Teach, train, guide, verify.

As we've discussed, that way you'll give your employees the authority and responsibility they've earned—and that will make them feel better about *their* jobs.

Speaking of streamlining, here's a very simple—yet very powerful—strategy.

THE 1 PERCENT ADVANTAGE

It's very hard to make massive gains in skill and performance and talent, especially overnight. But it is pretty easy to make tiny changes.

In 2009 Sir Dave Brailsford, a former director of British Cycling, was seeking funding for the program. He told the British government he could build its first-ever Tour de France winner in four years by using a strategy he termed "aggregate marginal gains." His plan was to break down each individual component that goes into making a world-class cyclist and cycling team, and improve each of those elements by 1 percent.

Not 5 percent or 10 percent or 20 percent, but just 1 percent.

Three years later Bradley Wiggins of Team Sky won the Tour de France and an Olympic gold medal. And for three of the next four years, Chris Froome of Team Sky won the Tour de France.

The "1 percent advantage" works incredibly well for one simple reason: Small improvements add up to a major overall improvement. Ever so slightly streamline your morning routine, the way you handle e-mail, the way you handle voice mail, the way you schedule appointments . . . and soon you can free up thirty minutes of your day so you can (you guessed it) do more of what you do best.

Keep this in mind, though: Most goal-setting advice that touts the power of incremental gains focuses on making small improvements over time in one skill or pursuit. For example, this week I'll try to do four pull-ups, then next week I'll shoot for five, then six . . . but of course I'll eventually run into a performance-improvement wall.

The 1 percent advantage focuses on breaking down all the component parts of a pursuit and then making a marginal but meaningful improvement to each one of those parts. You don't have to become phenomenally better at one task—you can just get a teeny bit better at a number of tasks.

If You're In a Relationship, 1 Percent Improvements Are Visible

Research shows that the person you marry can have a dramatic impact on your job satisfaction and career success. But beyond choosing your significant other wisely, there are plenty of things you can do to help your spouse be more successful—and better yet, those things can also make your relationship stronger.

Keep in mind the key word in that sentence is "do." Thinking and feeling are great, but action—the things you do, many of them small, each and every day—is everything. And what you do is give.

Not take, give.

Here are some of the things people who want to help their partners be more successful, and make their relationship stronger, do for each other. Make a tiny improvement in each area, and you'll be amazed by the cumulative effect.

Ask for a Little More Help

While it's relatively easy to ask for help with something practical, it's harder to ask when the help you need is personal. But as you know, when you ask for help, several things happen. You implicitly show that you respect the person giving the advice, that you respect their experience, skill, and insight. And you show that you trust the person, because by asking for help you make yourself vulnerable.

Asking for help shows other people that you respect and trust them. Isn't that a great way to make people feel?

Set a Little Better Example

Researchers at Washington University in St. Louis found that people with relatively prudent and reliable partners tend to perform better at work, earning more promotions, making more money, and feeling more satisfied with their jobs.

That's true for both men and women. "Partner conscientiousness" predicted future job satisfaction, income, and likelihood of promotion, even after factoring in the participants' level of conscientiousness.* Be a tiny bit more conscientious and not only will you benefit, but so will your partner . . . and your relationship.

Compliment, Recognize, and Praise a Little More Often

It's easy to recognize people who do amazing things. But it's very possible that consistent praise is one of the *reasons* they do amazing things.

People who work to build a successful marriage sometimes see the good in their partner before that person sees it in themself—and that can provide the spark that just might help their partner reach their true potential.

---

* Gerry Everding, "Spouse's Personality Influences Career Success, Study Finds," *The Source,* September 18, 2014, https://source.wustl.edu/2014/09/spouses -personality-influences-career-success-study-finds.

Allow a Little More Space and Privacy

Everyone shares. Everyone likes and tweets. Lives have increasingly become more open books. Over time, we've started to feel we have the right to know more about others than we ever did before. That includes our significant others.

But sometimes we don't need to know. Sometimes the best gift we can give is the gift of privacy, of not asking, not prying—yet always being available, if and when our significant other does want or need to share. It's not necessary to *know* in order to *care*.

Spend a Little More Time Searching for Opportunities Your Partner Has Missed

We all want to improve, to grow, to succeed . . . but sometimes we get so deep in the trees we fail to notice the forest.

Take a little more time to look for opportunities your partner might have missed. But it's not enough to know your partner's goals; work a little harder to help your partner achieve his or her goals. Sometimes that means helping to open a door that might otherwise have remained closed.

Find a Little More Happiness in Your Partner's Success

Great business teams win because their most talented members are willing to sacrifice to make others happy. Great teams are made up of employees who help one another, know their roles, set aside personal goals, and value team success over everything else.

251

And that's exactly how great relationships work.

Every great leader answers the question "Can you make the choice that your happiness will come from the success of others?" with a resounding "Yes!" So do people who want their partner—and their relationship—to be successful.

Be a Little More Sincere

Paying lip service is easy. Sometimes it's hard to show sincere appreciation for a thoughtful gesture, a kind word, or extra effort. Sometimes it's harder to show sincere disappointment—with others, sure, but also with yourself.

Want a more successful relationship? Celebrate a little more. Empathize a little more. Worry a little more. In short, be a little more human. Your partner fell in love with a person. Be a real person.

Try a little harder to change your partner's life.

Weigh the personal against the practical just a little bit more.

WHAT HATH LOVE TO DO WITH COMMUTING?

Seeking professional success can impact the success of your marriage (and vice versa). For example, according to one study, if one spouse commutes longer than forty-five minutes, that couple is 40 percent more likely to get divorced.

(There are some caveats to that finding. If you've already spent five years or more commuting more than forty-five minutes, then

---

you're only 1 percent more likely to get divorced than couples with short commutes—think of it as a 1 percent disadvantage. In all likelihood, that's because you've already worked through the practical and emotional issues involved. Plus, if one of you had a long commute before you began your relationship, then you're also a lot less likely to get divorced than spouses who start a long commute later in their relationship.)*

Plus, in practical terms a long commute might not be worth it. According to another study, economists determined that it takes a 40 percent increase in pay to make an additional hour of commuting time pay off, at least in terms of personal satisfaction and fulfillment.† A few dollars an hour more won't make you happy if you have to drive an extra hour every day to earn it.

Factor that in with the potential cost to your relationship and the personal considerations could definitely outweigh the practical advantages.

Try a little harder to look at the big picture. Professional success is just one factor in the happiness equation. Make sure you look at every factor—especially the health of your relationship.

---

* Erika Sandow, "Til Work Do Us Part: The Social Fallacy of Long-distance Commuting," *Urban Studies* 51, no. 3 (August 7, 2013): 526–43, http://journals.sagepub .com/doi/abs/10.1177/0042098013498280.

† Alois Stutzer and Bruno S. Frey, "Stress That Doesn't Pay: The Commuting Paradox," *The Scandinavian Journal of Economics* 110, no. 2 (June 2008): 339–66, http://onlinelibrary.wiley.com/doi/10.1111/j.1467-9442.2008.00542.x/full.

If It Improves a Relationship, Imagine How the 1 Percent Advantage Will Work Everywhere Else

I know.

"Dude," you're thinking, if you're a guy, "you just spent a bunch of pages telling me how to improve my relationship. Jeez!" And if you're a woman, you're thinking, "You just spent all those pages telling me how to improve my relationship. Great!" (Men, there's a lesson in there.)

Yes, I did. But it bears repeating, your relationship is one of the biggest drivers of happiness (or lack thereof). For all you results-oriented individuals—your relationship is also often one of the biggest drivers of professional success: People with relatively prudent and reliable partners tend to perform better at work, earn more promotions, make more money, and feel more satisfied with their jobs.

So there.

But just to humor the doubters, let's look at some relatively simple ways you can use the 1 percent advantage to improve just about any area of your life.

It's a basic process-improvement exercise: You take a task, break it down into its component parts, strip away what is unnecessary, and optimize what is necessary.

Examples?

The part: Dave Kerpen, the CEO of Likeable Local, hand-writes three thank-you cards every day on the train ride to work.

The benefit to the whole: "When my staff, customers, partners, investors, media, and others get my thank-you cards," he says, "they love them, and it cements my relationships with them. But the main reason I hand-write three thank-you cards every day is that it allows me to focus on others and transforms my mood from bad to good, from good to great, or from great to ecstatic. You can't be upset and grateful at the same time, and this practice puts me in a great mood—to have a great day—every single day."

The part: Edward Wimmer, the cofounder of Road ID, wears T-shirts to work . . . but he irons them.

The benefit to the whole: "Yes, I iron my T-shirts," Edward says. "I use this simple routine as a subtle reminder to myself that Road ID, like every company, needs a leader. Even in a super casual environment, the boss should look the part. Nothing says 'The buck stops here' like a neatly pressed T-shirt . . . right?"

The part: Multiple Grammy Award nominee Joe Satriani starts his day by reviewing his "ideas" list in his workbook: song ideas, production ideas, new guitar techniques, etc.

The benefit to the whole: "Also on the list," he says, "are books to read, subjects to research, art projects to undertake, marketing ideas, creative people to reach out to. I pore over the list, imagine following through on some of the entries, add new ideas, and eliminate those that no longer appeal to me. This helps me feel that I'm moving forward creatively and gets my priorities straight.

"Then I get to work!"

The part: Art Papas, the founder and CEO of Bullhorn, stops and says hello to anyone new he sees in the company lobby, asking if they have been helped and if they would like a cup of coffee.

The benefit to the whole: "I started doing that when we were a tiny company and didn't have a receptionist," Art says, "but as we grew and hired more people, I noticed that all the employees had started doing it—it's actually become part of our culture.

"It's a little thing, but it really sets the tone and makes people feel very welcome. I definitely think it's helped us win over customers and new employees."

The part: While it might sound counter to my premise, Dr. Marla Gottschalk, an industrial and organizational psychologist, often follows an antiprocess. "When a topic intrigues me, I become nearly obsessed," she says.

The benefit to the whole: "Even though most people feel it's most productive to prioritize and then stick to a set schedule," Marla says. "I readily shuffle my day when possible so I can stay in the flow. While going down the 'rabbit hole' may not work for everyone, it definitely works for me.

"Fortunately, I've worked for individuals who have said, 'Go ahead, take some time and explore that,' and their understanding was a gift that shaped my future."

The key to the 1 percent advantage lies in determining what you want to accomplish and how *you* work best—and then making small improvements that let you incrementally improve your focus, your process, and your rate of success.

All of which is incredibly motivating—and will definitely make you happier too.

You *Can Do Anything 1 Percent Better*

Now it's your turn.

Start by tackling something simple. If you want to improve on the amount of time it takes you to get ready in the morning (which ultimately will allow you to do more of what you do best), break your morning routine down into its component steps.

Start with potential problem areas. Do you sometimes have to hunt for your car keys? Find a place to always put them and then *always put them there*. (Hopefully my wife is reading this.) If you want to cut down on the number of trips you make to the grocery store, keep a running list on your phone and *always refer to it when you shop*. (Hopefully I'm rereading this.) If you sometimes go to meetings unprepared, don't just slot each meeting onto your calendar; set a thirty-minute alert to remind you to do what it takes to be the most prepared and smartest person in the room.

Every time you do something less well than you should, add that to your 1 percent improvement list. Better yet, figure out how to fix it on the spot and add that fix to your routine.

Then be proactive. Look at the tasks you most frequently perform, break them down into component parts, and ask yourself two questions about each of the steps required:

- Do I need to do this at all? (Often you don't. But if you do . . .)
- Do I know someone who does this better? (I guarantee you do.)

Then consider that person a pro and do what they do. Forget the whole "I am unique" thing. Forget the whole "But I need to express myself as an individual" thing. You can still do that . . . but do it in ways that count. If you can improve one small thing, and another small thing, and another small thing, soon your success will be all the individuality you need—because you won't be like anyone else.

You'll be *you*—the you that you really want to be.

Which leads us to a really interesting place.

CHAPTER 9

The Bottom Line

The bottom line is what *The Motivation Myth* is all about: getting past the fluff and puff and fire walks and achieving the goals you want to achieve.

Like most bottom lines, this one is clean and simple.

Don't tell me your goals. Don't tell me your dreams.

Tell me your plan.

And don't be afraid to dream big, because now you know how to plan big.

And never, ever forget that even the most successful people started out just like you.

Everyone starts at the bottom. Everyone starts out insecure and hesitant and uncertain. The only difference between incredibly successful people and the rest of us? They found a way to put aside their uncertainties . . . and try.

If you're in business, remember that underneath the Armani

and Wharton and name-dropping is a guy or gal just as nervous and insecure as you. Symbols of success are often a mask. The playing field is always more level than it seems.

One of the most fun conversations I've had in recent years was with NASCAR driver Ross Chastain (you met Ross earlier).

"The first time I went to Texas Motor Speedway," Ross told me, "was my fourth race in the Truck Series. Texas is an extremely fast, 1.5-mile track. I had heard that people run wide open at Texas. The first time out on the track I was all set to run wide open . . . and I lifted. I just couldn't help it. I came in, told the team the truck was a little tight [meaning the front end didn't want to turn at speed], they made some adjustments, and I went back out.

"I thought, 'Okay, now I need to run wide open.' But when I got on the back stretch my right leg started shaking . . . so I took my hand and pushed my leg down to keep the gas pedal floored. I basically ran that lap with one hand on my leg."

Here's a guy who today competes at nearly the highest level of his sport . . . yet when he first drove on a big track, he had to hold his leg down to keep himself from lifting his foot off the gas pedal. That sounds like something I would do, but a big-time racer?

Yep. Big-time racers have done it too.

If you have doubts or fears, you're not alone. Everyone else has, or had, the same fears. Take heart in that fact—and then hold your leg down and keep charging. You'll find you had nothing to be afraid of . . . and that you can overcome other fears you may have.

If you're feeling low, put your head down and focus on your process. You'll improve—and you'll gain the motivation you feel you lack.

Your dreams are important, but your plan is what will allow you to achieve your goals and live out your dreams.

Don't wait for motivation. Get started. Work your plan.

When you do, you'll find all the motivation you need.

INDEX

INDEX

INDEX

INDEX

INDEX

INDEX